HUMAN RESOURCES MANAGEMENT AND TECHNICAL CHANGES

Human Resources Management and Technical Changes

Dr. Shoeb Ahmad

KALPAZ PUBLICATIONS
DELHI–110 052

HUMAN RESOURCES MANAGEMENT AND TECHNICAL CHANGES
(*Management*)

Rs. 750

ISBN: 81-7835-259-1

Published in 2004 in India by
Kalpaz Publications
C–30, Satyawati Nagar
Ashok Vihar Phase–III
Delhi–110 052
E-mail: Kalpaz@hotmail.com

Lasertypesetting by : Shree Vaishnavi Creations, Delhi
Printed at: Mehra Offset Press, Delhi

Dedicated To My Parents

Contents

Preface

The science which deals with the problems and development of labour force for intensive studies relating to economic, social, behavioural and political aspects may be called Human Resource Management. Truly, it is concerned with the proper use of the human factor in business. In modern times, the term Personnel Management is called by different names, i.e., Personnel administration Industrial Management or Manpower Management, etc.

The present book aims to study all problems related with labour or personnel. It has been prepared strictly according to common core syllabus of human resource management. It provides basic information on manpower development covering the integrated approach for the study of management aspects depending on the specific physical and economic characteristics.

The primary objective of the study is to consider ways and means for overcoming various constraints such as environmental context emerging human resources and assessment of prospective technologies for playing particular attention to the technological design and innovation. In making clear the contribution of technological change to economic growth for identification of technologies, creation of productivity - all these factors were being assumed for technological advancement, alternative measures to the society, economic influence and political pressures.

In addition to the technological changes under constraint of manpower that follows different implication on the extended organisational structure as an instrument to accomplish the social goal.

In retrospect, there was no single model of modernized technology, but rather a cluster of concepts that provided vocabulary for modernization across many sectors of national economics. The list of question that follow at the end of each chapter would provide help to the students in understanding the contents of the chapter in better way. The questions have been carefully selected from the question set at different examination.

It has stressed on enhancement of the fact that it deals satisfactorily with all the latest topics prescribed in the human resource management. The treatment is exhaustive and analytical in nature. The cases have been appended at the end of the book that probes deep into the subject and furnishes valuable information which is enlightening. A list of questions has been added at the end of each chapter for the guidance of students, on account of these reasons I hope this book will be welcomed by the students and teachers of management classes.

I am thankful to everyone in my circle of educationists for getting inspiration to write such a book covering the latest syllabus of manpower development. I am always grateful to my parents for their support, guidance and inspirations for writing this book covering emerging topics of manpower development.

I am also thankful to my publisher Kalpaz Publications, New Delhi for publishing the book timely. Suggestions from the reader are most welcome to make the book useful for the students.

(Dr. Shoeb Ahmad)

1
Concept and Perspectives of Human Resource Management

CONCEPT

Human Resource Management/Personnel Management

Management of human resources is known as human resource management or personnel management. It is the part of management process which deals with the management of human resources. Personnel management is concerned with human problems of an organisation so that individuals can make their maximum contribution to accomplishment of common goals and at the same time attain social satisfaction. It is the process of binding people and organisation together so that objectives of each are accomplished.

"Personnel function is concerned with the procurement, development, compensation, integration and maintenance of the personnel of an organisation toward the accomplishment of the organisation's major goals and policies."

- E.P. Flippo

"Personnel management is that part of management function which is primarily concerned with human relationships in an organisation, its objective is the maintenance of those relationships which enable all those engaged in the undertaking to make their maximum contribution to the effective working of that undertaking."

—- Indian Institute of Personnel Management, *Calcutta*.

"Personnel management is the art of acquiring, developing and maintaining a competent work force in such a manner as to accomplish with maximum efficiency and economy the functions and objectives of the organisation."

—- Society for Personnel Administration of *America*.

"Personnel management is that aspect of management having as its goal the effective utilisation of the labour resources of an organisation."

Paul G. Hastings

The terms 'Personnel Management and Human Resource Management' are interchangeable and both allude to the same activities and processes. Human Resource Management is a modern terminology, which gained currency during the late 1970s. The American Society for Personnel Administration espoused to change its name to the Society for Human Resource Management.

Recent Changes in Personnel Management

There requires spatial and temporal change. But there are certain important factors that involve the growth of human resource management as discussed below :

(i) Radical Changes in Employees

This factor stresses on the performance of quality goods and services. That means to say that the performance is needed to become cost-effective and upgrade work methods. The first ingredient required is managerial skill where the second ingredient is motivation of members of the organisation (employees). These two factors provided consequence in cultural and economic fields by their respective performances.

(ii) Recent Attributes followed by Management

This change has occurred in realm of modern age and provided technical and economic devices to solve the problems arising in the management. Deviating from traditional views, the management is more conscious in the determination of manpower to the organisation. The conscious arises and brings plan benefits and security programmes in collaborated formations. Such formations throw light in solving the problems relating to management of the organisation.

(iii) Determination of Values in Social and Cultural Aspects

To derive better performance devices, the management has adopted familiar changes relating to laws, language, knowledge, beliefs, moral, values and norms of individuals following the increased relations between industrial productivity and motivation of employees. Thus, decision making summarises increased education that has led to high mobility and therefore a high turnover.

(iv) Incentives in Changed Policies Attracting to the Government and Labours

In earlier period, the management of the organisation had to face various issues relating to labour problems such as strike, lockout and wages, etc. But enacted various protective laws concerned with industrial safety, industrial disputes, payment of wages and compensation following the rules and regulations of the organisation. Such changes have been made for equitable justice to all without discrimination of caste, creed, colour and sex.

HRM : A Diagnostic Model

The recent decade, the function faces a variety of challenges from various sides by optimising some functional expenses subject to the conditions of employees to work as a team to enhance the customer satisfaction. They are creating various cross functional teams to examine the problems in a holistic way and to coordinate the efforts of concerned functions. The functions can be diagramatically defined as shown below :

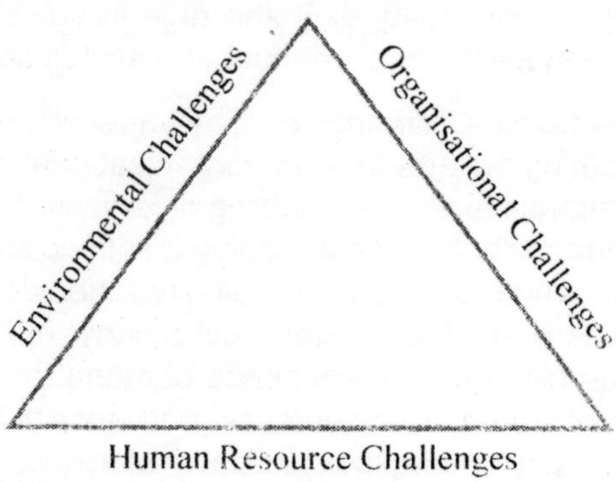

Environmental Challenges : They deal the external force affecting the performance of the enterprise and beyond the control of management. Some of these forces may be identified as increase in the competition due to (a) entry of multinational; (b) lower import duties; (c) collaborators becoming competitors and (d) providing multiple service.

For the consideration of mentioned facts as discussed above the following factors have been pointed by American Society for Training and Development (ASTD) as given below :

1. Training and Development
2. Organisation and Development
3. Organisation / Job Design
4. Human Resource Planning
5. Selection and Staffing
6. Personnel Research and Information Systems
7. Compensation / Benefits
8. Employee Assistance
9. Union / Labour Relations

The challenges also include market characteristics such as changes in economy, inflation, resource crunch, decline of traditional manufacturing industries, huge under-utilised capital (industries), restrictive, legislation, rapid changes in technologies—short shelf life of technology, dumping tendency of developed nations, unemployment in one hand, skill shortage in some area on the other, political instability, consumerism and ecological restrictions.

Organisational Challenges : They deal with the problems internally indicating the effects of the organisational challenges. In fact, every enterprise faces the following organisational challenges. Out of these, some challenges are being identified such as; (i) stiff demand of customers-cost, quality, delivery schedule, service etc.; (ii) impediments in acquiring latest technology; (iii) need of new employees due to consumerism hence demand for more salary / perks; (iv) resource crunch; (v) decreasing influence of Trade Unions; (vi) structure creating delays in organisational restructure; (vii) need for increased autonomy, demand for decentralisation (viii) pressure for downsizing; (ix) low utilisation of resources; (x) rise of individualism, team work is becoming difficult; (xi) aging work force, pressure forwards recruitment; (xii) organisational culture, norms, values; (xiii) difficulty in retaining experts and expertise, (xiv) paradigm shift from making products to providing services and (xv) old technology vs new technology and related problems.

Human Resource Challenge : In fact, Human resource addresses the decision most pertinent to the individual employees and seems quite challenging in respect of the following: (a) matching of individual and organisation needs more difficult; (b) rapid erosion in value and ethics; (c) demand for result orientation rather than activity orientation; (d) demand for more empowerment by employees; (e) losing talent due to luring by competitors (f) increased job insecurity and (g) demand for getting the best pay package.

The mentioned factors concerned with the given subject are found with (potent possibilities for both) external and internal complexities (for glimpse of the future in HRM). The complexities are found (emerging the challenges that are) to be diagnosed by making the devices based on philosophy, new interventions, systems and policies.

Although these functions relating to management would be changed in the case of HRM subject to the condition of creating new environment for new times.

Perspective

The present chapter of the book deals with different pertinent questions, such as : What is Human Resource Management and how it is helpful in achieving the organisational purpose? What is the significance of Human Resource Management and its relationship with other activities of the organisation?

After examining the various definitions, model and changes in Personnel Management we come across the following major characteristics as well as the exact role and place of HRM in the shape and operation of an enterprise.

1. Personnel management Human Resource Management is concerned with employees both as individuals as well as groups engaged in attaining organisational goals. It is also

concerned with behavioural, emotional and social aspects of personnel.

2. It is concerned with the development of human resources to the maximum possible extent so that they may be able to derive greatest possible satisfaction from their jobs. The development of human resources includes the basic elements like skill, knowledge, capabilities, potentialities and personality. The blending of all these attributes in an employee helps to attain corporate goals smoothly and effectively.

3. Human resource management covers all levels and categories of employees in an organisation. It includes workers, managers professionals, non-professionals, technical, non-technical, organised and un-organised workers.

4. Human resource management is applicable to all types of organisations. It may be government department, military organisation, industry, trade, non-profit institutions etc. human resource management is inherent in all organisations.

5. Human resource management is a continuous function George R. Terry has rightly pointed out, "It cannot be turned on and off like water from a faucet, it cannot be practised only one hour each day or one day in a week. Personnel management requires a constant alertness and awareness of human relations and their importance in every day operations".

6. Human resource management focuses on attaining the goals of an organisation, personnel working therein and society in an integrated and consolidated way. Organisational goals may include survival, growth, maximisation of value in addition to profitability, productivity, innovation, excellence etc. Goals of individual employees may include job security, high wage package, attractive fringe benefits, challenging work, pride, status, job satisfaction, recognition, opportunity of development, protection to the handicapped, reduction of disparities of income through minimum wage differentials, developing society in general through development activities, etc.

7. Human resource management is aimed at getting the willing co-operation of people for the attainment of desired goal.

8. Human resource management is not the sole responsibility of personnel manager but it is the responsibility of all the line managers and functions of staff managers in an organisation.

Thus, Human Resource Management is concerned with procurement and maintenance of capable and effective work-force, motivating employees individually and in groups them with the organisation in such a manner that the employees and the groups feel a sense of involvement and commitment to the organisation.

We can deal to above discussion by the following mathematical model:

Step I - IR (Industrial Resources)

Step II - MA (Managerial Action)

Final Step III - Re (Results)

Step I - Step II - Step III

For better manager,

R - M - Re = Me

Where R - M - Re denotes resource managerial result and Me is index of managerial efficiency.

∴ Me = Resources + Results.

Me = Resources + Results

Material resources | Human resources

Material resources ⇌ Human resources. Thus, in diagramatical representation.

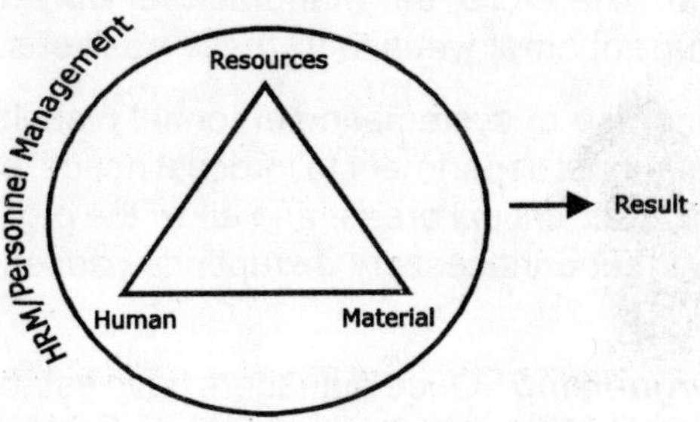

It does not, have a separate existence of own, Managerial functions include planning, organising, motivating and control. Since the above functions are common to all manager including personnel manager, and management involves accomplishing the results through people, it is rightly said that management is personnel management. A brief outline of various managerial functions is given below:

(i) Planning : Planning is a pervasive and continuous executive function involving complex processes of perception, analysis, conceptual thought, and communication. To get things done through subordinates, a manager must plan ahead. Planning is necessary to give the organisation its goals and directions to establish best procedures to reach the goals. Effective managers recognise that a substantial part of their time should be devoted to planning. For a personnel manager, planning means the determination in advance of a personnel programmes that will contribute to the goals meet, jobs descriptions and the determination of the sources of recruitment. The process of personnel plan involves three essential steps. First, a supply and the demand forecast for each job category is made. This step requires knowledge of both labour market conditions and the strategic posture and goals of the organisation. Second, net shortage and excess of personnel by job category are projected for a specific time horizon. Finally, plans are developed to eliminate the force shortages and excess. If shortage of accountants is projected over the next year, then the firm can begin searching for accountants through professional placement firm or through recruitment on college campus. Suppose that a manufacture of expensive jewellery is opening a new production facility next year it will need diamond cutting experts to start the opera Because of the specialized nature of this business it may not be possible to find diamond cutters whose technical background and experience are suitable. Therefore, the manufacturer may to have train and promote current employees to fill these positions.

Making use of systematic personnel planning programme it enables personnel department to forecast needs, plan for employee succession, staff-critical areas, and allow the organisation to meet its goals without unnecessary disruptions caused by shortages of personnel.

(ii) Organising : Once managers have established objectives and developed plans and programmes to reach them, they must develop and design organisation structure to carry out various operations. The organisation structure basically includes the following :

- Grouping of personnel activity logically into functions or positions;
- Assignment of different groups of activities to different individuals;
- Delegation of authority according to the tasks assigned responsibilities involved;
- Co-ordination of authority relationships horizontally and vertically in the organisation structure.

Organising is a never-ending process. All types of organisations need to be re-organised when goals and programmes are redrawn and activities also change.

(iii) Motivation : Plans must be put into effect by people, but how smoothly plans are implemented it depends on the motivation that people have to perform well.

Motivation as personnel function involves encouraging people to work willingly and effectively.

The personnel manager must inculcate in the workers a keen appreciation of enterprise policies. Motivation is not easy to achieve. Inspirational words alone will not do it. What a manager can try to do is to create a working climate which will encourage the desire to perform well. The key elements in such a work situation and its effect on the employee are:

- the degree to which the employee feels his personnel goals and those of the organisation are congruent;
- the employee's relationship with his co-workers and especially with his supervisor;
- the way in which his job helps him meet his present need of income and future security and does so in a manner that seems fair;
- the extent to which it enable him to feel adequate to his task and to gain a sense of accomplishment for jobs well done.

The personnel manager can motivate employees in an organisation through career planning; salary planning and administration, ensuring employee morale, developing cordial industrial relationship and provision of safety requirements and welfare of employees.

The personnel manager can motivate employees in an organisation through career planning; salary planning and administration, ensuring employee morale, developing cordial industrial relationship and provision of safety requirements and welfare of employees.

The motivational function poses a great challenge for manager. A personnel manager must have the ability to identify the needs of employees and the means and methods to satisfy those needs. Motivation is a continuous process as new needs and expectations emerge.

(iv) *Controlling :* Control is concerned with the regulation of activities in accordance with the personnel plans, which in turn have been formulated on the basis of an analysis of the fundamental goals of the organisation. Thus, control completes the cycle and leads again to planning. It is the observation and comparison of results with the targets and correction of results with the targets and correction of deviations that may occur. It consists of directives and measures to rectify any mistake in execution of plans. Controlling also helps the personnel manager to evaluate the performance of the personnel department in discharging the various operative responsibilities. Basically it involved personnel appraisal, industrial relations and evaluation of personnel administration audit.

In mathematically, we can discuss the above statement in this manner :

$$A + B + C + D = P$$

where,	A	denotes	personnel	management,
	B	"	marketing	"
	C	"	Financial	"
and	D	"	other managerial functions.	

- P depends upon; A, B, C and D.

TEST QUESTIONS

1. What is human resource management?
2. What are the characteristics of human resource management?
3. Explain different management functions.
4. Management of personnel is a basic responsibility of every manager. Discuss?
5. 'Management is personnel administration'. Comment.
6. Briefly outline the duties of a Personnel Manager.
7. Human resource management seeks to achieve personnel and social goals.

2

Environmental Context of Human Resource Management

Referring to environmental context to Human Resources, following the widespread adoption of an organization in developing countries, unlike India, it is sought to be extended to determine the sectorial conditions. However, such application is considered problematic as developing countries particularly in (India), South Asia, may be characterized by large informal sector, in complete structural transformation and high levels of poverty. The dualistic economic structure that characterizes these economics implies that very different conditions of employment prevail in the traditional and modern sectors. In view of these circumstances, Dreze and Sen (1980) [1] argued that the provision of environmental context in developing countries needs to be viewed from a broader perspective and essentially as an objective to be pursued through public means rather than as a narrowly defined set of particular strategies...(p. 16, emphasis in the original). Coincidentally, this definition was closer in spirit to the notion of Freedom from want putforth in the Beveridge Committee Report.

The articulation by Dreze and Sen of the alternative approach extended the scope of the term social security and several other researchers (Ahmad, 1991, Burgess and Stern 1999)[2] followed suit. The distinction between various connotations of the term social security has been maintained in the literature by naming the conventional ILO set of measures as protective (or formal) social security and the latter as promotional social security. The promotional category is rather broad and its scope is often ambiguous. A package containing both protective and promotional measures is often referred to as the wider concept of environment.

The distinction between various connotations of the term social security has as roots in fundamental differences in the development paradigm adopted and the concomital social policy implemented in the public domain. It is possible to identify two distinct though related paradigms that govern the formulation and implementation of social policy, viz, that of human resource development and human development.

(a) Human Resource Development

The human resource development paradigm is governed by the view that human beings constitute a means to higher productivity and income levels in the economy. In this paradigm it is assumed that individuals undertake to invest in themselves through education, health and nutrition in expectation of higher earnings. Hence investment in these sectors is largely in the private domain. Since education, health and nutrition are considered 'merit goods' the government has a role to play in ensuring minimum levels of consumption of these goods. However, this role is conceived mainly to be that of a facilitator rather than that of a provider. In keeping with this paradigm, provision of social security is confined rather narrowly to contingency related measures mainly for workers in the organized sector. The responsibility for such provision rests largely with the registered industrial firms and establishments with the role of the government being confined to providing an enabling environment comprising legal and administrative measures to ensure the provision of minimum levels of social protection to workers.

The protection of workers provides different factors allied with personnel functions. The personnel functions relates with personnel management, which may be classified into two sets as (a) Managerial and Operative.

These factors consider different properties such as planning, organizing, directing, motivating and controlling but the functions of these factors are used for managerial functions.

Managerial Functions

1. *Planning* - Planning is deciding in advance what to do in future. In the context of personnel management, it is concerned with manpower planning, studying turn over rate, forecasting the future requirement of personnel and planning for selection and training procedures, etc.

2. *Organizing* - Organizing involves the establishment of interrelationship within organization. It provides structure for the company for identifying the various subgroups, headed by individuals in managerial jobs as well as operative jobs.

3. *Directing* - Directing includes instruction to workers developing communication network, interpreting various industrial laws and integral workers.

4. *Motivating* - Motivating function involves motivation of employees through financial and non-financial incentives to increase productivity.

5. *Controlling* - Personnel department provides basic data for establishing standards; makes job analysis and performance appraisal, etc.

The second factor shows operative functions following the conceptions as mentioned below:

Operative functions

These are service or routine functions of personnel management. These are:

1. *Procurement of Personnel* - It covers human resource planning and forecasting and the process of recruitment selection, placement and induction of newly appointed employees.

2. *Development* - Development of workers and managers demand systematic programmes for employees training and management development, programmes of performance appraisal, promotion, transfer, etc. are also included under this function.

3. *Compensation* - Equitable remuneration in the form of wages, salaries, bonuses assume great significance, as compensation is the main motivator because our wants are satisfied with the help of money in the market for goods and services. Economic compensation involves varied and complex problems. It governs labour management relations.

4. *Integration* - Individual, social and organizational goals and interest are diverse and conflicting. They have to be reconciled and properly co-ordinated or integrated. Then only employees can offer their willing co-operation for united and joint enterprise. Democratic management reduces conflicts and assures effective morale and motivation.

5. *Maintenance* - It covers personnel activities relating to employee health and safety, favourable work environment, employee benefits and services, labour welfare work, worker participation in management, etc.

(b) Human Development

In sharp contrast to this viewpoint is human development, a term that is defined as the process of enlarging the range of people's choices. In this paradigm, human beings are considered ends in themselves. The provision of social secuity is not limited to protective measures of social insurance alone but extends also to programmes of social assistance as well as enhancement of capabilities. Thus, the provision of social assistance in the form of pensions for the aged and destitute are essential components of this paradigm. In keeping with this philosophy, the acquisition of minimum levels of education, health and nutrition are considered essential pre-requisites for enhancing social capabilities and constitute inalienable human rights. This in turn implies a dominant role for the government, which encompasses apart from a facilitator to that of a provider. The latter role acquires considerable importance in situations when access to social services is unequal and private provision is elitist in nature.

Additionally, since the human development paradigm relies on substained or participatory approaches to the enhancing of capabilities, it accords greater importance to the role of self-help groups, non-governmental and other community based organizations for the provision of social security. It is interesting to note that recent development literature has accorded importance to social institution in fostering what is termed as 'inclusive development' and advocates the use of a multi-pronged approach to enhance the capabilities of the poor.

(c) Socio-Economic Security

A more convenient way of referring the distinction between the conventional definition of social security and socio-economic securities. The distinction provides the concept of recent definition of securities Socio-economic security: Socio-economic security may be defined as constituting measures that enhance social capabilities, ensure economic security and enable the vulnerable sections of the population to survive. Thus, programmes for enhancing education, health and nutrition levels of the population, provision of statutory social security measures to workers in the organized sector, provision of measures to enhance the income levels of the poor through assets employment programmes and social assistance programmes, constitute the elements of our concept of socio-economic security. The agents that provide such security are spread over the government, firms, households and the community. The provision of minimum levels of income constitutes not only a necessity for survival but also an essential pre-requisite for the acquisition of education, health and nutrition that lead to enhancing of social capabilities as well.

(d) Distinction from Other Concepts

The concept of socio-economic security proposed here is also distinct from the conventional social security definition of ILO as it includes, in addition to ILO measures, various measures to enhance the social and economic capabilities of people. It is also distinct from the socio-economic security concept proposed by the ILO. IAMA 1999. Standing 1993)[3]. The ILO definition of socio-economic security comprises seven main components, viz. labour market security, employment security, job security, work security, skill reproduction security, income security, and representation security. Whereas labour market security recognizes the importance of appropriate macro policy in ensuring that high levels of employment prevail in the economy, employment and job harp on the regulatory framework to ensure protection against arbitrary dismissal and ensuring growth in the chosen career for employees respectively. Work security relates to the familiar provisions to ensure safety of workers and protection of workers against occupational hazards. Skill reproduction security lays stress on the opportunities for acquiring skills through apprenticeships and on-the-job training. The last two components, viz. income security and representation security, refer to protective labour legislation to ensure minimum wages, wage indexation, provision of social security benefits and the like whereas representation security pertains to the extent to which mechanisms for collective bargaining are present and are functioning effectively.

As is evident, though the ILO concept of socio-economic security recognizes the importance of macro policy and finding evidences the concept of stated organization (ILO) recognizes the importance of macro policy and overall employment conditions in ensuring socio-economic security, its scope continues to be governed by the needs and requirements for developing countries.

(e) Justification for Wider Concept of Socio-Economic Security

In fact, the socio-economic security cannot be assured in situation where there exists considerable unemployment. Similarly the situation arises, when workers are to be protected against illness and also adhered to any infection in health condition. Even that when they are stricken by minimum levels of literacy and numeracy as existing in different organized or unorganized sectors. Such event happens, due to reason of non-implementation of legislation towards organizational management.

Thus, there requires appropriate security policy initiative for workers, whether men or women.

Initiation of organized or unorganized sectors for employees, betterment.

In Indian economy, about 90 per cent of the workforce laid in unorganized sectors, where employees are considered to have low wages, uncertaintity of employment and underemployment and lack of other benefits like provident fund, dearness allowance, wage during holidays, maternity benefit and credit facilities, etc.

Finding such plight conditions our Government has enacted several legislations to make implementations of social security for employees betterment, even to women labourers to both organized or unorganized sectors. In order to follow extensive studies, several authors of socio-economic studies have given their focus and pointed out negligence towards the organizational management. In this regard, Avachat (1978)[4]; Mishra (2000), Basu (1978)[5] have explained various instances following an indication of non-implementation of Governmental policies that cause suffering to the employees of the enterprise.

The general downsizing of the workforce in any organization.

The following factors:

(i) Changed product mix and the paid disappearance of the requirement for traditional skills;

(ii) Changing location of production and obstructed mobility of workers;

(iii) Non-renewal of previously acquired specialization by workers;

(iv) Abrupt effort by the owners of non-labour resources to accommodate the entry of transnational capital in the firm;

(v) Managerial inefficiency in diversification of products to compensate the probable contraction in market faced by the firm;

(vi) Managerial apathy towards R&D and training for skill formation of workers;

(vii) Application of capital-deepening technical progress;

(viii) Downsizing of less efficient workers on the basis of intra-film efficiency parameters accepted by the owners of non-labour resources;

Then comes downsizing of the workforce not because of absolute intertemporal reducing productivity per worker. The scope of downsizing may crop up from relative productivity. The changes in technology and work organization, often complementing each other, have resulted in a shift in the nature of skill demand. The changing character of new technologies requires workers who can learn and adapt to these changes quickly and efficiently. Though the skill itself may not be "higher", the ability to master it quickly and use it productively calls for a high level of confidence and familiarity that favours the higher skilled (ILO), 1999, p.46). The relative obsolescence and degradation of a section of the workforce is manifested when there emerge a relatively advanced section of the manpower within the firm or even outside. The relatively advanced section is responsible to inventions and innovations. Employment of this advanced section in a fully operated (optimal capacity) firm will have a tendency to crowd out the section declared redundant.

Test Questions

1. Analyse the environment of human resource management in India.
2. What factors have hindered the progress of human resource management in India?
3. Analyse the environment of human resource management in India.

3
Corporate Objectives and Human Resource Planning

According to Louis Allen "Objectives are the goals established to guide the efforts of the company and each of its companents".[1] Objectives are key to effective planning. In fact, planning has no meaning unless it is related to certain well-defined objectives or goals. Objectives are not only useful in planning but also in other managerial functions like organising, directing and controlling. They are an important aid in decision-making in any area of business. Objectives are the ends towards which the activities of an enterprise are directed. It serves as benchmark of measuring the performance of various people working in the organisation and the overall effectiveness and efficiency of the organisation.

As the organisation determines its mission, objectives, desired future positions or destination that it wishes to reach, should be identified. Corporate objectives are defined as ends which the organisation seeks to achieve by its existence and operations.

Types of Objectives

Generally, big enterprises have both major and derivative objectives. Major objectives are set up for the entire organisation. They are broader in scope and are applicable throughout the enterprise. They are also known as primary objectives of the enterprise. Derivative objectives are derived from the major objectives of the enterprise. Every department draws its specific objectives in order to contribute to the major goals of the enterprise. They are also known as departmental objective and are subsidiary to the main objectives of the enterprise.

Time Dimension of Objectives

Since a business enterprise is a continuous entity, it must have both long-range as well as short-range objectives. Short-range objectives are set up for a short period of time, say upto one year, and long-range objectives are to be followed in the long-run. As a matter of fact, short-range objectives are devised to achieve the long-range objectives of the enterprise. They are more specific as compared to the long-range objectives.

Hierarchy of Objectives

The objectives of a company can be structured into a hierarchy. The objectives at the lower levels are the means for the higher levels. For example, a company may have the overall objective at the highest level to earn a fair rate of return by manufacturing and marketing specialised machine tools. If we go down the hierarchy, we shall find that the major objective followed by different departments focuses on creating the form of specialised machine tools. At the next level, there may be intermediate objectives concerned with manufacturing and assembling the major components. At the lowest level, the objective of the individuals consists of performing the detailed work on sub-component parts. The example illustrates the fact that the objectives at various levels in a company are integrated and follow a logical sequence as reflected by its organisation chart. Each operation has a specific objective which must contribute to the overall objective. In fact, there is the 'end-means' chain in the company. The objective at the top level provides the basis for setting the objective at the second level which in turn becomes the basis for thing the objective at the third level and so on. In other words, the goal at the fourth level is a means for the third level and so on.

Multiplicity of Objectives

It is wrong to presume that there can be only one objective of an organisation. To manage a business there is need to balance a variety of needs and goals. And this requires multiple objectives."[2]

Peter Drucker suggested the following eight key areas in which objectives must be set : (1) Marketing, (ii) Innovation, (iii) Human Organisation, (iv) Financial Resources, (v) Physical Resources, (vi) Productivity, (vii) Social Responsibility, and (viii) Profit Requirements.

Koontz and O'Donnell are also of the view that broad major enterprise objectives are normally multiple. "A business might include among its overall objectives a certain rate of profit and return on investment; emphasis on research to develop a continuing flow of proprietary products; developing publicly held stock ownership; financing primarily by earnings plough-back and bank debt; distributing products in foreign markets; assuring competitive prices for superior products; achieving a dominant position in an industry; and adhering, in all respects, to the values of our society."[3] Objectives in key areas enable the management : (i) to organise and explain the whole range of business phenomena by such objectives, (ii) to test the objectives in actual experience, (iii) to predict behaviour, (iv) to appraise the soundness of decisions while they are still being made, and (v) to set managers on all levels analyse their own experience and, as a result, improve their performance.[4]

Essential Criteria for Effective Objectives

Peter Drucker[5] has given the following guidelines regarding the objectives of a business organisation:

1. Objectives must be derived from "what our business is, what it will be and what it should be". Objectives, in other words, are the fundamental strategy of a business.

2. Objectives must be operational. They must be capable of being converted into specific targets and assignments.

3. Objectives must make possible concentration of resources and efforts.

4. There must be multiple objectives rather than a single objective.

5. Objectives are needed in all the areas where the survival of the business depends. The specific targets in any area depend on the strategy of the individual business. But areas

in which objectives are needed are the same for all business, for all business depend on the same factors for their survival.

What is Managing by Objectives (MBO)?

Ordiorne also stressed that MBO is not merely a set of rules, a series of procedures, or even a set method of managing, but it is a way of thinking about the management.

Management by objectives is also known as management by results and goal setting approach. Dale D. McConkey has preferred the term management by results and has defined it as an approach to management planning and evaluation in which specific targets for a year, or some other length of time, are established for each manager, on the basis of the results which each must achieve if the overall objectives of the company are to be realised. At the end of this period, the actual results achieved are measured against the original goal, i.e., against the expected results which each manager knows he is responsible for achieving.[6]

Benefits of MBO

Management by objectives calls for regulating the entire process of managing in terms of meaningful, specific and variable objectives at different levels of management hierarchy. Management by objectives moulds planning, directing and controlling in a number of ways. It stimulates meaningful action for better performance and higher accomplishment. It is closely associated with the concept of decentralisation because decentralisation cannot work without the support of management by objectives.

When applied consciously and systematically, it leads to the following results:

1. Stimulating the subordinates' motivation.
2. Providing a realistic means of analysing training needs and opportunities for growth on the basis of measurement of performance against accepted standards.
3. Improvement in productivity due to the fact that management team concentrates on the important task of reducing costs and harnessing opportunities rather than dissipating energies on less important matters.

4. Serving as a device for organisational control and integration.
5. Improved communication and organisation structure which helps in locating weak problem areas.

The Process of MBO

The process of managing objectives revolves around the setting up of organisation goals and the goals of various divisions and sub-divisions. It is a never ending process. The continuous nature of the process of MBO not only ensures sustained concentration of efforts towards organisation objectives, but also helps in modifying the objectives to suit the changed situation. The steps in MBO are described below.

(i) Setting of Objectives

The first step while installing the system of 'Management by Objectives' in an organisation is to establish verifiable objectives for the organisation and for various positions at various levels. In order to set the objectives of the enterprise, a detailed assessment has to be made of the various resources at its disposal. A market survey must be conducted to know what types of goods and services are required by the community. Proper forecasts should be made to estimate the demand and the business conditions in the country. This detailed analysis would lead to highlighting the desirable objectives of both long-range and short-range. An attempt should be made to set specific goals in various key areas on which the survival and growth of the business depends. These are the objectives which the top management will tend to achieve.

The top management must determine the objectives of every department. At this stage, the top management should discuss the objectives with the departmental managers so that a statement of agreed objectives may be evolved. Each department sets its both long-range and short-range objectives with the approval of top management. The process of setting objectives is repeated at lower levels of management.

(ii) Revision of Organisation Structure

When the goals for each individual are reset under MBO, there is a considerable change in the job description of various positions. This may call for a revision of the existing organisation structure.

The organisation charts and manuals should be suitably amended to depict the change brought by the introduction of management by objectives. The job description of various jobs must define their objectives, responsibilities and authority and the relationship with other job positions in the organisation.

(iii) Establishing Check-Points

Management by objectives ensures periodic meetings between the superior and the subordinate to review the progress towards the accomplishment of targets of the subordinate. For this, the superior must establish check-points or standards of performance for evaluating the progress of the subordinate. The standards should be defined quantitatively as far as possible and the subordinate must understand them fully. This practice should be followed by every superior for each of his subordinates and it should lead to key result analysis as targets or goals are represented in terms of results. The key result analysis should be reduced into writing. It should contain the following information.

(i) The overall objectives or the job of the subordinate.

(ii) The key results he must achieve to fulfill his objectives.

(iii) The long-term and short-term priorities of tasks he must adhere to.

(iv) The nature of information and reports he will receive to carry out self evaluation.

(v) The standards by which his performance shall be evaluated.

(iv) Appraisal of Performance

Informal performance appraisal or a subordinate is done by his immediate superior almost everyday, while the formal appraisal at periodic intervals, usually once or twice a year, and ensures that a thorough evaluation of a manager's performance is being done at least once or twice a year when the achievements are carefully analysed against the background of prevailling circumstances and given objectives. The design and format of the Performance Review Form will depend on the nature of the enterprise.

The important benefit of MBO is that it does away with the judgemental role of the supervisor. The performance of every individual is evaluated in terms of the standards or end-results clearly agreed to by the superior and the subordinate.

Human Resource Planning

Concept

The process of Manpower/Human Resource Planning is the key to the success of the organisation, if it is done carefully, cautiously and based on real and factual data available. It is process of determining how an organisation should move from its current manpower position to its desired manpower position. With the help of Human Resource Planning, Management strives to have the right number, the right kinds of people at right places at the right time to do the things which result in both the organisation and the individual receiving the maximum long run benefits. To understand precisely. Human Resource Planning consists in projecting future manpower requirements and the projections. Human Resource Planning is also called Manpower Planning, Employment Planning or Personnel Planning.

Human Resource Planning is a continuous process. It cannot be rigid or static; it is amenable to modifications, review and adjustments in accordance with the needs of the organisation or the changing circumstances. In the words of Coleman, "Manpower planning is the process of determining manpower requirements and the means for meeting those requirements in order to carry out the integrated plan of the organisation."[7]

Objective of Human Resource Planning

1. To ensure optimum use of Human Resources existing in the organisation.
2. To forecast future requirements for human resources to know it future needs so as to maximise the future return on investment on human resources.
3. They should develop procedure and techniques to determine the requirements of different types of human resources over a period of time.
4. To link human resource planning with organisational planning.
5. By anticipating the surplus and shortage of human resources

and by creating these imbalances in time, management can reduce labour costs over staffing under utilisation of talent, etc.

6. To anticipate the impact of technology on jobs and human resources.

7. To determine the levels and nature of recruitment and training.

8. To estimate the cost of human resources and housing needs of employees.

9. To produce, a sound basis for the development of personnel to make an optimum use of available talent.

Importance of Human Resource Planning

1. Human Resource Planning creates awareness about the right man for the right place because man is required in relation to work and it is basic to the requirement of manpower planning that this elementary, but fundamental principle is adhered to.

2. It ensures that adequate number of persons are selected and trained well in advance to full future job vacancies in the organisation.

3. Human Resource Planning, identifies existing/manpower gaps so that available training programmes may be developed in terms of their quality and quantity.

4. Provision for replacement of personnel can be made through human resource planning.

5. Human Resource Planning facilities the expansion and diversification of business in respect of assessing future requirements of the company expands or new units set up.

6. Human Resource Planning is helpful in effective utilization of technological progress.

MANPOWER PLANNING PROCESS

The manpower planning procedure has the following steps:

STEP I. Forecasting Manpower Requirements

There is no doubt that these sophisticated forecasting techniques are of considerable value when dealing with large-scale manpower planning, but for organisational units simpler methods can be used and are often more effective. For the forecast to be useful, it has to be made category-wise depending on the tasks that has to be carried out and the special qualification, training or experience required. There is no point in estimating that an organisation will require 50 men in the next five years unless it is estimated at the same time how many of them should be accountants, or engineers or chemists and so on. Therefore, the forecast has to be in terms of divisions, departments or functions.

The forecast also has to be aligned to the organisation's hierarchical structure. In other words, it is necessary to estimate not only the number of people in various functional categories that will be needed over the plan period, but also the levels at which they will be needed. Say, five managers it would be necessary to know how many of these should be senior level managers how many middle level and how many junior level.

Growth of establishment is necessitated by the expansion or diversification programmes and also by the addition of new specialist functions necessitated by changing technology or increasing complexity. A company may find it advisable to create a research and development department or quality control unit or introduce mechanised data processing. Any such activity will create new manpower demands.

Expansion and diversification plans take a long time to nature. So, there is usually sufficient time to create and implement a manpower plan to meet the consequential manpower demands. Unfortunately, whereas a great deal of attention is paid to the requirements of money, machinery, raw materials, etc. hardly any thought is given to manpower requirements.

Besides growth of establishment, additional staff requirement will inevitably arise due to the people leaving the organisation for various unpredictable reasons. Some estimate has to be made of this number. It is a generally accepted practice in planning to reduce the area of uncertainty. Therefore, the number of people who will definitely leave having reached the retirement age should first be taken into account. After that, unpredictable turnover should be assessed. This has to be based on past experience. Development may take place in the future as a consequence of which past experience will not necessarily apply. In assessing this factor, there is no substitute for judgement based on knowledge of the environment.

For instance, the turnover may fall if there is industrial recession. If there is industrial expansion, particularly in the same industry, then the turnover will almost certainly increase. The extent to which this happens depends on the standing of an organisation. If it is well established and well managed, then new units will inevitably look upon it as a possible source of trained, efficient and experienced personnel.

STEP II. Preparing Manpower Inventory

Manpower inventory or manpower audit refers to the analysis and assessment of current human resources. The purpose is to know the size and quality of personnel available within the organisation to man various positions. Manpower audit will indicate the unutilized talent and the gaps that exist in the present manpower. The inventory of various skills (skill inventory) may be indexed to ensure that all available talent has been included.

STEP III. Identifying Manpower Gaps

Net human resource requirements or manpower gaps can be identified by comparing demand forecasts and supply forecasts. Such comparison will reveal either shortage (deficit) or surplus of human resources. The objective of human resource planning is to bring together the forecasts of future demand and supply. The result of the effort will be to pinpoint shortages both in number and in kind to highlight areas where overstaffing may exist (now or in future) and to keep abreast of the opportunities that exist in the labour market to hire good people either to satisfy current needs or to stockpile for the future.

STEP IV Formulating Manpower Plans

In this step appropriate and detailed policies, programmes and strategies for recruitment, selection, training, promotion, retirement, replacement etc. of existing and new employees to meet the forecasted needs are made. Such plans are designed to ensure a continuing supply of trained manpower to take over jobs as they fall vacant. Efficient manpower plans are required to meet effectively the manpower needs of the enterprise.

Test Questions

1. What do you understand by objectives and its types?
2. What is the criteria for effective objective?
3. What is managing by objectives?
4. Explain the process of MBO?
5. What are the objectives of manpower planning at enterprise level.
6. What do you understand by human resource planning with suitable illustrations?
7. What is manpower planning? Why it is necessary? Discuss the various steps involved in it.
8. What are the characteristics of human resource planning?

4

Job Analysis and Role Description

Concept

Job analysis is a collection of data. A job is consist of task, duties, responsibilities which as a whole is regarded as an assignment to individual employees. It is a procedure by which the facts with respect to each job are systematically discovered. It is also known as job study or work study.

According to Flippo, "Job analysis is the process of studying and collecting information relating to the operations and responsibilities of a specific job. Job analysis provides information both for the job holder. It involves the breaking up of a job into its basic elements and studying them in detail to obtain all pertinent facts about the job. It provides information about job contents, job duties personnel qualities required for the job.

Objectives of Job Analysis

1. Work simplification.
2. Establishment of work standards.
3. Support of other personnel activities.

Job Analysis Information

The job analysis provides the following information:

1. Job identification which includes job title.
2. Significant characteristics of a job including location, physical setting, supervision, union jurisdiction, hazards, etc.
3. What the typical worker will do?
4. What materials and equipments the worker uses.
5. Proforma of job duties.
6. Required personnel attributes.
7. How the job is performed.
8. Job relationship.

Uses/Advantages/Benefits of Job Analysis

1. It helps to improve efficiency due to better placement and frequently suggests methods for improvements.
2. Job analysis information gives the description and specification. On these basis, students can be given exact counselling in making their career.
3. Job analysis helps in improving the design of jobs and work methods. It aids in analysing work-processes and work simplification.
4. For a new trainee, induction programme is designed to impart some knowledge regarding the work and organisational environment.
5. Job analysis helps in devising the training and development programmes for employees.
6. Job analysis gives us two important segments, i.e., job description and job specification which are job factors. On the basis of these factor job evaluation process is done.
7. It provides a basis for manpower planning and for recruitment and selection of personnel. It reveals the nature and qualities of people required for a job.
8. It assists management in the proper allocation of authority and responsibility by describing the duties of each job and the interrelationships among jobs.
9. It facilitates job evaluation and performance appraisal which are necessary for wage determination, for appraising the working conditions and promotions and transfers.

10. By facilitating the matching of employee skills with job requirements, job analysis helps to improve job satisfaction, motivation and morale of employees. Absenteeism and turn over of the personnel can be reduced.

STEPS IN JOB-ANALYSIS OR PROCESS OF JOB-ANALYSIS

There are basically four steps involved in the process of job analysis. They are:

(1) Objectives of Job-Analysis

Before any activity is undertaken, one must know the objectives of that activity. The process of MBO is prevalent everywhere. First, set the objective of job-analysis, accordingly, collect the information. Because job-analysis is done for different purposes, i.e., job evaluation, training, promotions and transfers, recruitment and selection and performance appraisal. The purpose will lead the best information because stress will be laid down in gathering the required information which would achieve the objective of job-analysis.

(2) Selection of Representative Position to be Analysed

There are numberous of jobs in an organisation and each job is followed by a number of position. Each position of a job cannot be analysed because it is complicated and time-consuming. So Analyst has to decide what position of a job will be analysed as a representative.

(3) Information Gathering

Under this phase of job analysis, decisions on certain related issues are first taken, such as: what type of data is to be collected (which depends on the end use of information, and the time budget constraints: what methods are to be employed for data collection, e.g., observation interview, questionnatires, checklists etc.): and who should collect the data (e.g., trained job analysis, supervisors, or job incumbents). Then the required information is duly collected.

(4) Information Processing (Job descriptions, job specifications, and job standards)

This information needs to be processed so that is will be useful for human resource department and other departments. The immediate application of this information transforms it into job descriptions, job specifications, and job standards, 'Job description' explains the duties, responsibilities, functions, operations, working conditions, and other aspects of job. 'Job specification' describes what the job demands of the incumbent or employee who does it and the human skills or characteristics that are required to successfully perform the job, such as experience, training, education, and physical and mental abilities. 'Job performance standards' serve two functions: (i) They become target for employee efforts, (ii) Standards are criteria against which job success is measured. Without standards, no control system can evaluate job performance. Job performance standards are developed from the information collected for job analysis, and actual employee performance is then measured against them. Job standards are a key part of any control system.

METHODS OF GATHERING JOB INFORMATION FOR JOB ANALYSIS

(1) Job Performance

Under this approach, the job analyst actually does the job under study in order to have direct exposure and get first-hand experience of and information about the actual tasks, physical demands, and environmental conditions of the job. This method is appropriate in circumstances where skill requirements are low and therefore can be learnt by the analyst quickly and easily. However, this is a crude and time-consuming method and is not suitable in case of those jobs which require extensive training before performing upon them.

(2) Personnel Observation

Under direct observation approach, the analyst simply observes a worker or group of workers doing a job. Sometimes he reviews films of workers engaged in doing the job. Without interfering, the analyst records the what, why, and how of the various parts of the job. During a complete cycle of performance of a job, he also observes the working conditions and the hazards involved. Information is collected on the sequences of observed behaviour. Usually this information is recorded in a standard format. This approach is most often used for the analysis of jobs that consist largely of repeated manual operations over a relatively short time cycle. This method is simple and data collected are accurate. It may be preferred when analyst wants to confirm or remove doubt about the data collected through questionnaires.

(3) Personal Interview

This method of collecting information is most reliable and result-oriented. Without this step, the job information will be incomplete. It is greatest promise of completeness, accuracy and better utilisation of time. It is used as a prime method of data collection.

It may be noted that without personnel Interview and observation, the information so collected will be incomplete, unreliable and inaccurate. Personal observation and interview are more or less complete and accurate. Interview is a very psychological phenomenon. It is very difficult to get true information from the employees as they conceal the fact due to certain psychological and social problems. It depends on the tactics of the job-analyst that how he can motivate them.

(4) Questionnaire Method

In this method, questionnaire is prepared and questions are asked from the employees. The main problem with this method is non-response and inaccurate response by the employees. As this method is incomplete and insufficient for job analysis still questionnaire method is good for making base for the interview.

(5) Records method

Personnel department maintains the records of the facts regarding the job and the job holders. The analyst collects the information from the record maintained by the personnel department.

(6) Motion Study Method

Under this method, the speed of an individual worker in performing some job and time consumed therein are both noted. Similar examinations being performed on other individuals doing the same work, the results obtained are compared. Such a study of speed and time helps in job analysis and classification of the workers.

ROLE DESCRIPTION

A man's behaviour is judged from his role in the society. A man performs many roles at a time in the society. He may perform his occupational role of a worker, family role of a parent or of a child, social role of an office bearer of an institution or club. He may be a buyer, a seller, a subordinates, a supervisor, a manager, a leader at the same time and each role has a different behaviour.

Roles may be on-the-job or off-the-job but a man may perform more than one role at a time.

The role is the most complicated organised response patterns of which a human being is capable. The role perception, i.e., what they think and what others expect from them in a given situation, guides the activities of a person.

A role set is the combination of surrounding roles which affect a particular role. For example, a supervisor in an organisation comes across with other persons—officials and subordinates persons expect a particular role, different for each one from a supervisor. They expect a way in which the supervisor should act. We may say it role expectations. Different expectations collectively make up the role set for the job. This role set arises partly from the nature of work itself.

A manager (or other person), interacting with someone else needs to perceive three role values : (i) Job perception, i.e., perception of own role as required by the function being performed. In other words, what he expects from himself, (ii) perception of others' role, i.e., what he expects from others, and (iii) others' perception, i.e., what role others expect from him as a manager. It is very clear that one cannot satisfy the needs of others till he realises what others expect from him. If the manager thinks of role perception of the job in a different way than what workers think of role expectation of that job, the motivation will be poor and may lead to inefficiency. Communication between them may become difficult because there are no talking about the same thing in the same way. For example, a manager think the autocratic manners the best way of performing the job, while others expect participative role.

A person is said to be in role conflict if expectations of a role are materially different or opposite because one expectations cannot be met without rejecting the other. Where role expectations are not clearly defined, there is a role, ambiguity. In such situation people are not sure how he should act. Where role conflict and role ambiguity exist there is diyfunctional results which shows a declive in job satisfaction, and unfulfilment of needs.

Employees, generally are satisfied with their jobs when their roles are defined clearly, i.e., there does not exist role ambiguity. It helps the person to understand what others expect from him or what he should act. It also helps to understand others with whom he is to interact.

Test Questions

1. What do you understand by job analysis? Discuss its ones.
2. Define job analysis. What are its objectives? How it is different from job evaluation?
3. Describe the techniques used for analysing jobs.
4. What are the steps involved in the analysis of job? Explain.
5. What do you mean by role establishment?

5
Attracting and Selecting Human Resources (Recruitment and Selection)

As the process of Manpower Planning is finalized the next step is to hire the personnel according to the requirements. Now various questions arise to be answered, where to hire when to hire, who is to hire, hiring should be from within or outside, what should be the media or source and finally how they should be hired? All these questions are responded properly when a company is having suitable and appropriate personnel policies and procedures. Recruitment has been regarded as the most important function of Personnel Administration because unless the right type of people are hired, even the best planning organisational charts and control system would not do much good. Recruitment makes it possible to acquire the number and types of people necessary to ensure the continued operation of the organisation

Meaning of Recruitment

Recruitment forms the first stage in the process which continues with selection and ceases with the placement of the candidate. Recruiting makes it possible to acquire the number and type of people necessary to ensure the continued operations of the organisation. Recruiting is the discovering of potential applications for actual or anticipated organisational vacancies. In other words it is a 'linking activity' beginning together those with jobs and those seeking jobs.

Flippo views "Recruitment as both positive and negative factor. Positive factor because it is the process of searching for prospective employees and stimulating and encouraging them to apply for jobs in an organisation. Negative because it rejects a good number of those who apply leaving only the best to be hired."

Thus the company must have its policy on Recruitment, Selection and placement. It must also have its policy regarding Interviewing, induction and psychological tests which form an important base of selection.

Steps in Recruitment Process

According to Femulras, recruitment process is comprised of five elements namely as—recruitment policy, a recruitment organisation, developing sources of recruitment, techniques used for utilising these sources and a method of assessing the recruitment programme.

Now we discuss these one by one.

1. Recruitment Policy

The Recruitment Policy determines the objectives of the recruitment and provides a framework for implementation of the recruitment programme in the form of procedures. The success or failure largely depends upon the ability and efficiency of the employees. Recruitment policy should be very sound so that capable and efficient employees are hired only. A good recruitment policy possesses the following features.

1. Recruitment policy must be fair and flexible.
2. The selection of employees must be strictly in accordance with the merit.
3. It strikes a good balance between organisational and individual needs.
4. All selection must be made at the central place of the enterprise,
5. Few posts must be authorised by higher officer.
6. The qualification, experience, terms of service, salaries etc.

must be determined well in advance.

7. The whole process of the recruitment must be completed by a senior, responsible and reliable officer.

2. Recruitment Organisation

Recruitment organisation in relation to recruitment practices differ from one organisation to another. Under centralised recruitment organisation Personnel Department (at the head office) performs all the function of recruitment. On the other hand in case of decentralised recruitment each department or unit performs all the functions and carries out its own recruitment.

Merits or Advantages of Centralised Recruitment

(i) It helps in better utilisation of experts available with the company.

(ii) It reduces the administrative cost by consolidating all recruitment activities at one plan.

(iii) It ensures rational, effective and suitable placement of candidates.

(iv) It ensures uniformity in recruitment and selection of all types of employees.

(v) It enables the company to have single or uniform procedure in the fields of selection, transfer and promotion.

Demerits/Disadvantages

(i) Delay in recruitment where a department is in urgent need of employee.

(ii) Job recruitments of different units is some times not known to the control office.

3. Sources of Recruitment

Before the process of recruiting the applicants start, it should consider the most likely source of the type of employees it needs. Some company try to develop new sources, while most only try to tackle the existing sources they have. Basically, we may divide the sources as internal and external.

(A) Internal Sources

Internal sources of recruitment means promotion of employees from the lower rank to higher rank. Most of the companies have a policy of promotion from within. Vacancies other than at the lowest level are filled up by promoting the personnel to the higher office. Thus, there is a chain of promotion that can be filled from these lowest in ranks by giving them training to make them eligible for higher position in the organisation. Practice of internal recruitment leads to a healthy and progressive atmosphere, lower cost of training and a high rate of labour turnover. This source of recruitment is generally adopted to fill vacancies of middle and top personnel. Lowest recruitment is generally from external sources.

(B) External Sources

Every enterprise has to top external sources also for various position because all the vacancies can't be filled through internal recruitment. The present employees may be insufficient or they may not fulfill the specifications of the jobs to be filled. Although external recruitment is expensive and time consuming but provides wide choice. The various external sources of recruitment are—

i. Direct Recruitment.

ii. Media Advertisement.

iii. Employment Agencies.

iv. Campus Recruitment.

v. Casual Callers.

vi. Recommendations.

vii. Head Hunters.

(1) Direct Recruitment

In direct recruitment a notice is placed on the notice board of the enterprise specifying the details of the jobs available. It is also known as recruitment of factory gate. The practice of direct recruitment is generally followed for filling casual vacancies requiring unskilled workers. Such workers are known as casual or badli workers and they are paid remuneration on daily-wage basis.

This method of recruitment is very cheap as it does not involve any cost of advertising vacancies. It is suitable for filling casual vacancies when there is a greater rush of work or when a number of permanent workers are absent.

(ii) Media Advertisement

Advertisement in newspapers or trade and professional journals is generally given when qualified and experienced personnel are not available from other sources. Most of the senior position in industry as well as commerce are filled by this method. The advantage of advertising is that more information about the organisation, job description and job specification can be given in advertisement to allow self screening by the prospective candidates. Advertisement gives the management a wider range of candidates from which to choose. Its disadvantage is that it brings in a flood of response, and many times, from quite unsuitable candidates.

(iii) Employment Agencies

Employment exchanges which are controlled by the Government are regarded as a good source of recruitment for unskilled, semi-skilled and skilled operative jobs. In some cases according to law compulsory notification of vacancies to the employment exchange is required . Thus, the employment exchanges bring the job givers in contact with the job seekers. However, in the technical and professional areas, private agencies and professional bodies appear to be doing the most of the work. Employment exchange and selected private agencies provide a nation-wide service in attempting to match personnel demand and supply.

(iv) Campus Recruitment

Jobs in industry have become increasingly technical and complex to the point where college degrees are widely required. Consequently, many big organisations maintain a close liaison with the educational institutions for recruitment to various jobs. Recruitment from educational institutions is the well established practice of thousands of business and other organisations. For example, organisation which require large number of clerks or which seek applicants for a continuing apprenticeship programme usually recruit from vocational institutes.

(v) Casual Callers

The job seekers casually and voluntarily visit the offices of well-known or high wage companies to deposit their applications in data bank, sometimes they mail also. Some companies prepare a waiting list of such unsolicited visitors, especially to fill temporary and lower level job. This is an expensive source, but this source is uncertain and the applicants need a careful screening because they mention a wide range of abilities in their application.

(vi) Recommendations

Applicants introduced by friends and relatives may prove to be a good sources of recruitment and, indeed, many employers prefer to take such person because something about their backgrounds is known.

(vii) Head Hunters

Those who keep tap and search for individual presently working and holding position and job profile in another companies.

4. Methods or Techniques of Recruitments

Recruiting methods or techniques are the means by which an organisation established contact with potential candidates, provides them necessary information and encourages them to apply for jobs. Various methods or recruitment have been classified into a three-tier model as follows:

1. Direct Method (Contact)

Direct recruitment involves travelling recruiter is scouting employee contacts, internships, manned exhibits and waiting lists. In scouting, skilled and semi-skilled employees are recruited from Vocational Schools and Industrial Training Institutes. They also exchange views with the students, clarify their doubts stimulate them to apply for jobs. Sometimes employees are told to contact the publies to inform about, Internships give the student a unique opportunity to experience a company first hand and also provide managers with an excellent opportunity to further assess the student's capabilities and potential. Manned exhibits involve sending recruiters to seminars and convertion. Some organisation use waiting lists of candidates who have indicated their interest in jobs in person, through mail or over telephone.

2. Indirect Method (Inform)

Advertisements in newspapers, journals, radio and television are used to publicise vacancies in which only Box No. is given without identifying the firm.

3. Third Party Methods (Attract)

Various placement agencies and other parties can be used to attract job seakers. The important ones: like public and private employment agencies, profession search firms, professional associations, Educational Institutions, Trade Unions, Head Hunters, etc. friends and relation of existing staffs and deputation method can also be used.

5. Recruitment Programme in India

1. Internal Sources.
2. Direct Recruitment.
3. Media Advertisement.
4. Campus Recruitment.
5. Labour Contractors.
6. Recommendations.

With recruitment, SC & STs are given reserve quota. Defence personnel and displaced persons from other countries are also given preference. In state level enterprise 'sons of the soil' are given preference. But for managerial cadre competition is on all India basis.

The foremost objective of management recruitment in India is to find the best man to achieve organisational goals. Recruitment Programme should be evaluated periodically. The criteria for evaluation may consists for cost per applicant, applicant rates, performance appraisal, tenure of stay, etc. The organisation has to keep an eye over a particular method that whether it is useful to attract best quality or not. Results gathered from the evaluation helps to make necessary improvements in the recruitment programme.

Selection

It is the process of choosing the prospective candidate who can match best with the job profile as well as can adjust best with the organistion culture.

Selection divides all the applicants into two categories (a) suitables (b) unsuitable. It may be described as a process of rejection because generally more candidates are turned away than are hired. It is different from recruitment. Recruitment technically precedes selection.

Selection Procedure

It is a series of successive hurdles or barriers which an applicant must cross. These hurdles or screens are designed to eliminate on unqualified candidate at any point in the selection process. This technique is called "successive hurdles technique."

Steps in selection Procedure: The following are the mentioned process:

(1) Application Blank

It is a traditionally widely used device for collecting information from candidates.

Many large companies use two sets of application forms. One seeks to obtain basic personnel data about educational qualifications, training, experience etc. to determine whether the candidate possesses the basic minimum recruitments. If the candidate is selected on the basic of the form, he is given a more detailed application form aimed at gaining deeper insight.

Generally an application form seek information in the following areas :

1. Personal data such as age, sex, marital status, height, weight etc.
2. Family background such as father's and brother's occupation.
3. Educational background including training.
4. Employment record including details about previous employment if any and present employments.
5. Names and address of a few, usually three persons other than relatives to whom reference can be made.
6. Membership of professional organisation.
7. Reasons for seeking job in the organisation.

(2) Preliminary Interview

This is often called 'courtesy interview' which is simply a matter of good public relations. Based on job description and job specification some of these candidates are declared as obvious misfits.

(3) Reference Check

The applicant is asked to mention the names and addresses of his former employers and also of two or three persons known but not related to him in the end of the application blank. The purpose of reference check is to know the (detail facts) reality about the candidate.

The most fruitful method of checking references is through face to face interview with the referees.

(4) Physical Examination

Sometime it is also conducted because it is an optional steps depends upon the type of job to be done by the applicant. It's basic objective is (1) to know the physical capability of the applicant (2) to present the organisation with communicable diseases (3) to protect the organisation against unwarranted claims under worker's compensation laws.

(5) Psychological Tests

It is devised to measure the psychological characteristic of individual applicants for a position. It is an objective and standard measure of a sample of human behaviour. It acts on the principle that individual differ from one another by degree.

A variety of psychological tests are used as selection tools.

(a) *Intelligence Test* : to measure, individual's capacity for reasoning verbal comprehension,. numbers vocabulary, word processing etc.

(b) *Aptitude Test :* to measure talent or capacity to learn the job if he's given adequate training.

(c) *Achievement Test :* to ascertain whether individual actually knows what he claims to know.

(d) *Interest Test :* to predict whether a candidate is interested in a particular job or not.

(e) *Personality Test* : to measure personality characteristics as emotional stability, tolerance for conflict, capacity to get along maturity, etc.

(6) Employment Interview

The purpose of employment interview is to final out the candidate's mental and social makeup and to know the qualities prevailed by him make him suitable for a job in the concern. It must be conducted in the friendly environment. The questions should better be asked on the basis of job specification. It is face to face communication and involves a brief personnel contact with the candidate to judge his suitability for the job.

(7) Final Approval

If the candidate successfully overcome all the tests given above, he is declared selected. An appointment letter is given to him mentioning the terms of appointment, pay scale, designation on which selected, etc.

Steps in selection procedure are flexible. They may vary from organisation to organisation or in some organisation from job to job. All depends upon the size, nature and objective of the enterprise also on the nature of the job and job description of the enterprise. Initially appointment is generally made on a probation of one or two years. After satisfactory performance during the period the candidate is finally confirmed to the concerned job.

Test Questions

1. What do you understand by 'recruitment'? Explain the precess of recruitment.
2. Discuss critically the various sources of recruitment for executives.
3. Describe the nature and importance of employee selection. Explain in brief the steps involved in selection procedure.
4. Discuss the importance of psychological tests and interviews in employee selection.
5. What are the methods of recruitment used in India?
6. Write notes on:

(a) Recruitment Policy.

(b) Recruitment Practices in India.

(c) Types of Interview.

(d) Group Discussion.

7. Distinguish between Recruitment and Selection. (B.Com Bharathiar, 1994).

8. What is meant by selection procedure? Indicate the overall selection process step by step. (B.Com. Bharathiar, 1994).

6

Induction and Socialisation

Simply induction or orientation means the act of introducing a person into a new job, work group or an organisation. It can be defined or explained as—

(i) Induction is helping to new recruits straight into company's commotion.

(ii) Rotating them rapidly to different functions.

(iii) Exposing them to every aspects of the company's business, culture.

Once, an employee is selected and placed on an appropriate job the process of familiarising him with the job and the organisation begins. This process is called induction or orientation.

The purpose of orientation is to make the new entrant feel at home and develop a sense of pride in the organization and commitment to the job. Induction is the part of socialisation.

Michael Armstrong - "Orientation is the process of receiving and welcoming an employee when he first joins a company and providing him the basic information that he needs to settle down quickly and happily and start work."

Purpose of Induction

An Induction/Orientation Programme is designed to achieve the following objectives:

(1) to develop confidence in newcomers about the organisation and in himself so that he may become an efficient employee.

(2) to promote a sense of belonging new and loyalty in the new comers regarding the organisation.

(3) to ensure that the newcomers do not form false impression regarding the new place of work because first impression is the last impression.

(4) to give the newcomers necessary information such as location of cafeteria, toilets and locker room, rest periods and leave rules etc. and also about the organisation's structure, products and norms.

(5) to foster a close and cordial relationship between the new-comers and the old employees and their supervisors.

(6) to lessen or avoid the cost of replacing the worker in the early impressionable period because of lack of information or incorrect business impression.

Contents/Information of Induction Programme

A formal induction programme should provide information concerning the following:

1. Brief history and operations of the company.
2. Company's Organisation Structure.
3. Location of depts and employee services.
4. Products and services of the company.
5. Personal Policies and Practices.
6. Rules, regulations and daily work routines.
7. Standing Orders.
8. Benefits and Services for Employees.
9. Opportunities for Training, Promotions, Transfers etc.
10. Safety Measures.

Suggestions for Effective Induction Programme

1. Induction is the most significant part of human side so first of

all a new employee should be introduced with his superiors and co-workers and should also know what they expect with him.

2. The new employees should be introduced with the company's rules and regulations as well as his specific role.
3. New employees should be allowed sufficient time to adopt to a work situation before job demands are increased.
4. Provide on the job instruction and counselling.
5. New employees should be sponsored or directed by an experienced worker or superior who can respond to questions and keep in close touch during the early induction period.

Meaning and Definition of Socialisation

When a new employee joins a new organisation, the human resource department helps him in learning the values of the organisation. Therefore socialisation is a process of learning and adaptation. In a broader sense it is the sharing of norms, values, beliefs and work culture of the organisation imparted to the new incumbent. This is a process which continues throughout the career of the employee which involves transfer, promotion or demotion.

Objectives and Importance of Socialisation

The major objective of the socialisation process is to develop a homogeneous and congenial work atmosphere in the organisation. So that the employees could be productive and helpful for the organisation.

Socialisation Process

The socialisation process involves following stages:

(1) Defining Appropriate Behaviours **:** Every organisation has a particular culture that defines the appropriate behaviour for the organisation. Culture is a set of beliefs, values and set of behaviour patterns. These are shared and transmitted by the members over years. Although the rules and regulations are not written, yet these are exchanged among the members by special language, shared patterns of work and a particular behaviour pattern.

Values are the criteria of measurement. These tell as to what is right and what is wrong, good or bad, desirable or undesirable. The role and the behaviour of the employees is guided by these.

Thus, the values and beliefs held by the members of the organisation define the appropriate behaviour of the new incumbent.

(2) Work-group Norms : The members of a particular organisation develop common work group norms. Thus, there grow certain expected behaviour patterns of the members. They care for each other in case of need, threat, attack loss or any kind of festinity etc.

(3) Roles : Roles are the expected behaviour patterns of a certain job. An employee has to play different roles in different situations. He has to be a boss with his subordinates, a pear with his colleagues and be a seller with outsiders.

This is a fact that the norms, values and roles are quite inter related when an employee works in his organisation, this is his role. This role is performed according to the certain norms and values of the orangnisation. These concepts are related to the socialisation process.

(4) Learning the "Do's" and "Don'ts" : The organisations expect that the norms must be accepted by all members. Without this acceptance, new employees will have no commitment and loyalty to the interests of the organisation. They will not be helpful for the organisation and will never be accepted as the members of the organisation.

Therefore, the successful socialisation of an employee means that he has a perfect knowledge of the "do's" and "don'ts" of the organisation, where he works.

Test Questions

1. What is induction and what is its importance?
2. What information induction programme should provide and what suggestions are needed to make it effective?
3. What do you understand by socialization and its processes?

7
Training and Development

Training and Development are the Human Resource Development Programme which help to ensure that the organisation has the people with the skills and knowledge it needs to achieve strategic objectives.

Through training and development programmes we train

- new employees to the level of performance required on their job, and
- develop the abilities, competencies of the existing staff.

In simple terms, training refers to imparting of specific skills, abilities and knowledge to an employee for doing a particular job.

It fills the gap between

- What someone can do?
- What he should be able to do?

It is an organised procedure which enhances the skill, knowledge and variety of competencies.

Training : Training is the act of increasing knowledge and skill of an employee for doing a particular job.

- by Flippo

Management Development is growth oriented. It is a process by which managerial personnel acquire not only skills and competency in their present job but also capacities for future managerial tasks of increasing difficulty and scope.

It provides for people to do better in existing job and prepare than for greater responsibilities in the future.

It builts on strengths and helps to overcome the weaknesses and also ensure that the organisation has the expertieese it needs.

Since the nature of the job is constantly changing due to:

(i) Changes in environment.

(ii) Changes in organisational priorities.

(iii) Changes in goals and strategies.

(iv) Changes in technology, and apart from the changes some new opportunities and challenges may come to meet all these changes so we need new knowledge based and continuously developed competencies and attitude of our employees.

Development

Development means that employees acquire not only skills and competency in their present jobs but also capacities for future managerial tasks.

- by Flippo

Need for Training

In modern corporate world, the necessity or requirements of training may arise for different reasons as follows:

1. To adapt or adjust existing methods and techniques to changing environment or needs.
2. To match the employee specification (qualifications, skills, knowledge, abilities etc.) with the job requirement and organisational needs, i.e., to fill the gap between the two.
3. To improve the efficiency and effctiveness or work performance of the employees—to secure employee effectiveness in order to maintain organisational viability in changing environment and increasing competition.

4. To achieve higher productivity.
5. To create skills of coordination, integration, and adaptability to requirements of growth, diversification and expansion.
6. To prepare employees for internal mobility, i.e., for higher level jobs.
7. To reduce supervision time, minutes spoilage of wastage of materials, time, and energy.
8. To develop potential abilities of workmen.

Challenges

- Make learning one of the fundamental values of the organisation.
- Use training to bridge the gap with external world.
- Initigerate training into initiatives for change management.
- Link organisational, operational and individual training needs.

Benefits/Payoff of Training and Development

(i) it provides the organisation with the skill and experteese it needs to achieve its strategic objective/goal.

(ii) to improve efficiency and effectiveness of the existing employees.

(iii) it help people to develop their inner potential so that organisation could meet its future human resources requirement in terms of both quality and quantity from within the organisation.

Use Retraining

- to continuously upgrade employees skill.
- create a system to evaluate the effectiveness of training.
- regard training as an investment workout total vers as benefits (dividend).

Types of Training

A training programme may be comprising of the following types:

(a) On the Job Training

It refers to the training provided while working on a job to increase the knowledge and skills of an employee for latter performance on the job. Employees may be taught the correct methods of handling equipment and machines used in a job. Such training helps to reduce accidents, waste and inefficiency in the performance of the job.

(b) Off the Job/Class-room Training

Off the job training means where in the training is imparted away from the workplace. The training may be imparted at the company class-room or places which are owned by the company, school, college, university or associations which have no connection with the company's real work place. It is classified as Lectures, Conferences and T-Group Training.

(c) Refresher Training

It is designed to an update the knowledge and experteese of the existing employees. Short term refresher courses have become popular on account of rapid changes in science and technology.

(d) Orientation Training

After recruitment induction or orientation training helps to adjust newly appointed employees to the work environment. Every new employee needs to be made fully familiar with his job, his superiors and subordinates and with the rules and regulations of the organisation. It is also known as pre-job training.

(e) Promotion Training

It involves training of existing employees to enable them to perform higher level jobs. Employees with potential are selected and they are given training before their promotion, so that they do not find it difficult to shoulder the higher responsibilities of the new positions to which they are promoted.

(f) Induction Training

Induction means the introduction of newly appointed employees to their jobs, to their fellow workers and to the organisation.

Induction training pitches fresh recruit straight into company's commotion. Rotating them rapidly to different functions and exposing them to every aspects of company's business culture.

(g) Remedial Training

Such training is designed to correct the mistakes and shortcomings in the behaviour and performance of employees. Remedial training should be imparted by people who have knowledge of human nature and industrial psychology.

(h) Safety Training

Training provided to minimise accidents and damage to machinery is known as safety training. It involves instruction in the use of safety devices and in safety consciousness.

PROCEDURE OF TRAINING PROGRAMME

Determining the need and priorities for training

Stage (I)

A training programme should be established only when it is felt that it would assist in the solution of specific operational problems. The important step is made thorough analysis of the entire organisation, its operation and manpower resources available in order to find out the trouble spots where training may be needed.

Identification of training needs must contain three types of analysis:

(i) Organisational analysis

(ii) Operations analysis

(iii) Man analysis

(i) Organisational Analysis

Centres primarily on the determination of the organisational goals. In terms of its resources for allocation and utilisation, growth potential and its environment. Its purpose is to determine where training emphasis should be placed within the organisation.

(ii) Operations Analysis

It help to decide what the training should consist of, requiring a study of what a person shall be taught if he is to perform his task with maximum effectiveness.

(iii) Man Analysis

Reviews the knowledge attitudes and skills that he must require and what allocation in his behaviour he must make if he is to contribute satisfactorily to the attainment of organisational objectives.

Stage II. Establishment of Training Objectives

On the basis of the training needs the training objectives are to be determined. After the formulation of training objectives the decision relating to when, whom, how and by whom are to be decided.

Stage III. Development of Training Programmes

In many cases, training of employees of particular departments is separated organisationally from the personnel department. Line supervisors must be alert to recognize training problems that exist in their departments. They also participate in creation and emplementation of special training programmes to solve specific problems in their units. Management must review and approve the training plans and the training budget.

Stage IV. Make up of Training Programme

Every training programme includes trainees, trainers or instructors, a training period and training material. A trainee should be trained for the kind of job he likes and is fitted to perform. In this respect, training is closely related to the selection of the personnel.

After the preparation of the trainee, the instructor is to be prepared. Qualified instructor may be obtained from inside or outside the organisation. However, many insiders, are not good instructors because they may not possess the ability to teach to skill.

The trainer should explain and demonstrate the operations step by step and should allow the trainees to repeat these operations. He should also encourage questions from the trainees in order to be sure that the trainees understand the job.

The length of training period depends upon the skill to be acquired, the trainee's learning capacity and the training media used.

To maintain interest and secure maximum accomplishment, no single session should last longer than two hours. Now the questions arises whether the training should be given during working hours or after the working hours.

There is always the need for training material. The training section must prepare the training material with the help of line supervisors to be used for different jobs. The training material should be distributed among the trainees well in time so that they may come prepared in the class and may follow and clear their doubts by as king from the instructor.

Stage V. Evaluation of Training Programme

(i) Determining whether a programme meets its goals.

(ii) Identify strengths and weaknesses in the training process.

(iii) Calculate the cost-benefit ratio of a programme.

(iv) Determine who benefited the most from a programme and why.

(v) Establish a database for future decision about the programme.

METHODS OR TECHNIQUES OF TRAINING

The most popular training methods used by organisations can be classified as either on-the-job or off-the-job training.

On-the-Job Method

On-the-job means while working on a job. Numerous training methods may be used while the man is engaged in the process of productive work. These on the job training methods are suitable for all levels of personnel. Some of the major techniques used under on-the-job training may be discussed briefly as follows:

(1) Job Instruction Training (JIT)

It is a popular form of on-the-job training. It is also known as training through step-up-step. In this method the trainee is taught the necessary skills to perform on a regular job. The trainee learns under the guidance and supervision of superior or an instructor. The trainee learns by deserving and handling the job. Therefore, it is called learning by doing. Following are the methods of training on job Instruction Training.

Coaching : Under coaching method the employee is trained by his superior. It involves direct personnel instruction and guidance, usually with extensive demonstrations and continuous critical evaluation and correction.

Position Rotation : The trainee is periodically rotated from job to job instead of sticking to one job so that he may acquire a general background of different jobs.

Understudy : Under this method a superior gives training to a subordinate as his understudy. The purpose of under study is to prepare someone to fill the vacancy caused by death, retirement, promotion or transfer of the superior.

(2) Apprenticeship Training

In this method, theoretical instruction and practical learning are provided to trainees in training institutes. In India the government has established Industrial Training Institute (ITIs) for the purpose. Generally a stipend in paid during the training period. Thus it is an 'earn when you learn' scheme.

(3) Pre-employment Training

It is the training by an organisation in which job seekers are tested and instructed in employment fundamentals without pay. In the programme, training lasts upto some hours in all, such as from 100 hrs. to 360 hrs. in all. It includes mannual (i.e., physical elevences and skill) testing alongwith instruction (education) in tool use and manufacturing process. Trainees are rated on their willingness to work as well as on job aptitude.

(4) Off the Job Training

Off the job means the training which is imparted away from the work place. The training may be imparted at the company class room or places which are owned by the company, school, colleges, universities or associations which have no connection with company's real work place.

Off-the-job training means class-room training which are classified as under :

(i) Lectures.

(ii) Conferences.

(iii) T-Group Training

(i) Lectures

Lectures are of vital importance when specialised knowledge regarding facts, principles, theories, concepts, attitude and problem solving abilities are to be taught. Lectures are delivered by specialised trainers or form a superior on the specific topics. The Lecture method is very useful for the organsiation, in the sense that if decreases or reduces the cost of training and development. It is a peculiarity of lecture method that it is very active method of teaching and especially when a very complicated topic, technical special or complex knowledge is to be imparted. The method can be used when very large groups are to be trained within a short time. Lectures are usually enlivened with discussions, case-studies, film-shows, role playing and demonstration. Audio-visual play more important role and enhance their value. Its success depends on the able and specialised lecturers, interests of participants and purpose of training which may turn out to be more interesting and effective than any other method.

(ii) Conferences

In this training system the individuals confer to discuss the issues of common interest to each other. It is a formal and participative meeting, conducted according to organised plan in which leader seeks to develop knowledge and understanding by obtaining considerable amount of oral participation of the trainees. It lays emphasis on active participation of the members involved. Through this method earning is facilitated by building up the ideas contributed by confesses.

Conference is of three types: (i) Directed Discussions in which trainer guide the discussion in such a way that the facts, principles, or concepts are explained. (ii) Second in training conference, the instructor gets the group to pool his knowledge and past experience and brings different opinions for a particular problems. (iii) It is as seminar in which the trainer or leader defines the problem encourages and ensures full participation of the conferenes.

(ii) T-Group Training

It is called popularly as T-Group where T-Stands for technical. This method is usually comprised of association, audio-visual aid and planned reading programmes. Members of this type of training programme are interested to receive new techniques and ideas pertaining to their own vocations. This can only be possible when there is regular supply of profession journals and informal social contacts or gathering and members are kept inform of the latest development in their particular field. To make this type of training a success, audio-video aids, records, tapes and films are generally used conjunction with other conventional teaching methods. Two things are most required things, i.e., planned and supervised reading and technical publication and the latest journals kept in the library for the use of trainees.

Test Question

1. How will you identify training needs of an organisation? Describe the process of training.
2. Explain various methods of training employees, pointing out the merits and demerits of each.
3. Explain the various methods commonly used in training and development programmes in various organisation.
   (B.Com. Bharathiar, 1994).
4. Explain whether and how the effectiveness of training programmes can be evaluated.
   (IGNOU, 1989)
5. Differentiate between training and development.
6. Define training. How are training needs determined in an industrial organisation?
7. What are the principles to be kept in mind while designing a sound employee training programme?
   (MBA, Delhi, 1985)

8

Performance Appraisal and Potential Evaluation

It is the process of obtaining, analysing and recording information about the relative worth of an employee. Although Performance Appraisal and Potential Evaluation are used synonimously, but Performance Appraisal is a wider term than Potential Evaluation. The Potential Evaluates the different traits of the employee by comparing the qualitative factors such as nature of individual, physical and mental ability etc. whereas Performance Appraisal Evaluates the performances of an employee by comparing the quantitative factors such as quantity of output and rejected output, standard of work, etc.

Thus, is Potential Evaluation the stress is on 'what he is'. While in Performance Appraisal, the emphasis is on 'what he does' and 'what potentialiy does he possess'?

Performance Appraisal

Performance Appraisal is a systematic, periodic, and so far as humanly possible, an impartial rating of employee's excellence in matters pertaining to his present job and to his potentialities for a better job—

Flippo.

Potential Evaluation

Potential Evaluation attempts to systematic, periodic and, so far as humanly possible, an impartial retain of an employee's excellence in matters pertaining to his present job and to his potentialities for a job.—

Edwin, B. Flippo.

Purposes of Performance Appraisal

- to improve job performance and identify the potentialities for other work.
- to identify the need and areas for further training of the employees.
- to assist in determining promotion and transfer policies.
- to reduce the grievances among the employees.
- to make the compensation plans more scientific and rational.
- to help in proper placement of the workers after the completion of their training.
- to facilitate research in personnel management.
- develop positive relations in between superior subordinate.

Q. What is appraisal? How appraisal is to be implemented?

1. Appraisal is a two way discussion between the appraisor and the appraisee.
2. It is an open document that both appraisor and the approve agree and sign.
3. It is a plan for future.
4. It is a constructive criticism of the performance and personality of the appraisee in the immediate past.
5. It's meeting without emotions being involved.

Important Aspects of Appraisal Programme

1. Determining Objectives

It is advisable to set the objectives of the performance appraisal. There may be two objectives of performance appraisal, either to evaluate the actual performance of individual on the job or to determine the potential of individuals for higher jobs or both. Generally, the supervisors are asked to the judgement in both the areas.

2. Establishing the Standard of Performance

The standards must be very clear and objectives should be easily understood and measured. The performance standards are discussed with the supervisors so as to involve them in standards setting. Being more practical in the job and its factors, he will give certain factors which are to be incorporated, the weights and points to be given to different job factors. After finalising the performance standards, they should be indicated on the Appraisal from which are later used to appraise the performance of the employees. Provisions are also made for the things which are beyond control of the human resources that is called 'MBE' 'Managing By Exceptions'.

3. Communicate Standards to Employees

Until and unless, the employees are informed, what is expected of them, it is difficult to guess what is to be done, how much is to be done. Feedback should be the tool as a confirmation that they have received the communication regarding Performance Appraisal-Standards. The feedback should be from subordinate to manager. It also ensures that communication has been received in the same sense and spirit.

4. Selection of Appraiser

It should be decided who will be the appraiser? In most situation the rater or earlier is immediate supervisor of the men to be appraised he is most familiar to them and their work and he is considered to be the most able man to appraise them well. But there are certain limitations of one man's appraisal, so some companies try to obtain two or more ratings on each employee. There are certain other companies which constitute a committee consisting of the representatives of the employees and supervisors and the specialists of the personnel department.

5. Measurement of Actual Performance

The performance measurement crieteria should be developed, how to measure, what to measure. The measurement should be according to job factors which have been settled before hand. Like quality and quantity of work, dependability, personality development and traits and Behavioural Aspect four sources of information are frequently used to measure actual performance, Personal observations, Statistical Reports, Oral Reports and written reports. Arbitrarily measurement of the traits is to be avoided.

6. Compare Actual Performance with Standard

As the measurement of actual performance is over it is compared with predetermined standards. The employee should be appraised and judged of his potential for growth and advancement. The comparison will show that some employees are lagging behind or deviating from the performance standards, some may exceed the standards and some may just meet the standards. Attempts are made to note deviations between Standard Performance and Actual Performance.

7. Consultation with Supervisor and Union Representatives

The rater after completing the rating process discusses the situation with supervisor and union representatives and defines the performance level and incorporates the valuable suggestions any, advanced by them.

8. Holding Feedback Sessions

The final step in an appraisal programme is to hold feedback sessions where the subordinates performance and progress are discussed and plans are made for initiation of corrective action or for any development that is required.

Limitation of Appraisal

Performance appraisal may not yield the desired results because of the following deficiencies.

(i) If the factors included in the assessment are irrelevant, the result of potential evaluation will not be accurate.

(ii) Different qualities to be evaluated may not be given proper weightage in certain cases.

(iii) Some of the factors are highly subjective like initiative and personality of the employees, so that actual evaluation may not be on scientific lines.

(iv) Supervisors often do not have critical ability in assessing the staff. Sometimes, they are guided by their personal emotions and likes. So the evaluation are likely to be biased.

Effective Appraisal System

An appraisal system to be effective it needs to be based on the following elements.

(i) The performance appraisal system should be performance based, uniform and non-variable, fair just and equitable. It should be ensured that the appraisers are honest, rational and objective in their approach, judgement and behavioural orientation.

(ii) Periodic goal setting.

(iii) Periodic or Annual Assessment of performance in term of such goal.

(iv) Analysis of the achievement of these goals -

  (a) identifying facilitating and inhabitating factors in relation to the achievement of goals.

  (b) development of action plans for overcoming inhabitating factors and strengthening the facilitating factors.

(v) The results of the performance appraisal must be immediately communicated to the employees especially when they are negative so that they may try to improve their performance and also they will be able to know where do they stand.

(vi) Periodic review of behaviour which contributes to management effectiveness.

  (a) action plan for achieving such behaviour.

(vii) Identification of development needs.

  (a) action plan-training and related activities.

Methods of Performance Appraisal

Performance appraisal methods may be broadly divided into two broad categories:

Traditional method and Modern method.

Under Traditional method are

1. Ranking methods.
2. Paired comparison method.
3. Forced distribution method.
4. Graphic rating scales.
5. Checklist method.
6. Critical incident method.
7. Confidential report method.
8. Man to man or factor comparison method.
9. Field review or Interview method.
10. Group Appraisal method.

Under Modern Method there are -

1. Assessment Centre.
2. Behaviourally Anchored Rating Scale.
3. Appraisal by Results (MBO).

(1) Ranking Method

It is a simple process of placing employees in a rank one after the other from highest to the lowest based on their overall performance on the job. This method is best, provided the number of employees is very small 'the work done is of a quantitative nature.'

The greatest objection of this system is that in practice it is very difficult rather undesirable to compare a man with the all other men in the organisation because human personality in itself is very complicated. The man differs from one another and can't be compared to all. It is very difficult for the rater to say 'good' or 'bad' to any person. Another difficulty with this system is that it doesn't indicate the degree of difference between the first man and the second man.

(2) Paired Comparison Method

Comparison is made on the basis of overall performance. The number of comparisons to be made can be decided on the basis of the following formula.

$\frac{N(N-1)}{2}$ where N is the no. of persons to be compared. Exp., if there are three workers namely x,y,z, in a job group, the pair can be determined by this formula.

This method is easier and simpler than ranking method. But it is subjective because *appraisal is not based on specific job* related performance. Secondly, it becomes very cumber some when the no. of employees to be rated is large.

(3) Forced Distribution Method

Under this method the raters rate the man on overall job performance. This systems based on the presumption that employees can be divided into five points scale of outstanding above average, average, below average and poor. In this system the appraiser is asked to distribute the employees into these categories in such a way that about 10% of the men are in group 'outstanding', 20% above average, 40% average, 20% below average and 10% poor.

(4) Graphic Rating Scales

It is a numerical scale indicating *different degrees* of a particular trait. The rater is given a printed form for each employee to be rated. The form contains several characteristics relating to the personality and performance of employees. Intelligence, quality of work leadership skills, judgement etc. are some of these characteristics. Rating scales are of two types viz. continuous and discontinuous. In continuous scale the degrees of a trait are measured in nos. ranging from 0 to 5 whereas in a discrite of discontinuous scale appropriate boxes or squares are used.

(5) Check List Method

This is also known as questionnaire method. In this method for the accomplishment of job, an index of necessary merits are prepared. Evaluator reads that list to a person and these merits which are found in him are (+) marked while those which are not in him are (-) marked. If he is doubtful about a merit, is marked with (?)

This system has the possibility of partiality as evaluator does the work himself. Secondly, each department or work needs separate forms as nature of work, character and responsibilities have vast differences.

(5) Critical Incident Method

In this method, such specific events are selected which are related to his job like overcoming with anger at the working time, declination to co-operate, suggestion for improvement in work procedure, prohibition of future training. These incidents are weighted and ranked in order of frequency and importance. In this method there is much scope of biased decision. If the critical incident doesn't happen, it will be difficult to rate the employee. It is also difficult for the superior to decide what is critical and exceptional.

(7) Confidential Report Method

In this method each employee is rated confidently by one or more senior officers for his performance. A confidential report by supervisor is a major determinant of the subordinate's promotion and transfer. This report deals with the years work and general opinion of the rater towards the employee. The main problem with this method is that it is not data based and the appraisal is done on the basis of impressions.

(8) Man to Man Comparison or Factor Comparison Method

Under this method, certain factors are selected for the purpose of comparison such as leadership, initiative, dependability, reliability etc. After that a 5 point master scale is designed for each factor by the rater. A scale of men is also created for each factor putting the best at the top and worst at the bottom, an average man in the middle of the scale and one below the average and one above the average. Then each rater is compared with the man in the scale and certain score for each factor are awarded to him, each man is compared with the key man in the scale for each factor at a time, instead of comparing the man as a whole. This system of measurement is used today in job evaluation being known as 'factor-comparison method.' Though it is highly useful in measuring job, it has very limited use in measuring people, because designing of the moniter scale is a complicated task.

(9) Field Review Method or Interview Method

Under this method supervisors are interviewed by an export from the personnel department. The export questions the supervisor to obtain all the pertinent information on each employee and makes a record. They are also asked to suggest measures for improvement in employees performance. These notes are sent to supervisor concerned for his approval or modifications. Thus the employee is rated as a whole. If the interviewer is competent and the supervisors co-perates with the interviewer this system may be very useful even for large enterprises.

(10) Group Appraisal Method

Under this method, a group of evaluators assesses employees. This group consists of the immediate supervisor of the employee, other supervisors having close contact with the employee, work head of the department. and personnel experts. This group determines the stand and of performance for the job, measures actual performance of an employee analyses the causes of poor performance and offers suggestions for improvements in future.

Modern Methods

It is important in the context of new technology for quality development.

(1) Assessment Centre Method

An Assessment Centre method is a multiple assessment of several individuals performed simultaneously by a group of trained evaluators using a variety of group and individual exercises. Typically individuals from different departments are brought together to spend two or three days working on individual or group assignment similar to ones they will be handling if they are promoted. Evaluators evaluates, deserve and rank the performance of all the participants both collectively and individually by using simultion techniques computer simulation method, business games, case studies and in-basket exercises.

Now let us see-how these techniques are helpful in our potential development.

(a) Computer Simulation Method

The computer permits training in which the trainee interacts directly with the computer programme for exp., the trainee can read question directly from the computer screen, supply the answer via the keyboard, and immediately receive a grade or a corrected answer. This immediate feed-back can be quite beneficial, especially if the trainee must master one unit of material before procedure to new materials.

(b) Gaming Simulation or Mgt. Games

These are mgt. development exercises in which participants are given background information instruction about rules and condition and perhaps roles to play. One example would be complex computerised games which are frequently played on an electronic computer that has been programmed for a particular game. In such a game, each team makes decisions on various matters such as fixation of price, level of production, inventory level, and so forth. Since each team is competing with others, each firm's decision will affect the results of all others. All the firm's decision are fed into a computer which is programmed to behave somewhat like a real market. The computer provides the results, and the winner is the team which has accumulated largest profit. In the light of such results, strength and weaknesses of decisions are analysed. Another example (not computerised) is a consensus exercise in which members of group make individual decisions and then attempt to improve *their individual scores through effective group interaction*. The trainees are divided into groups or different teams. Each has to discuss and arrive at decisions concerning such subjects as production, pricing, research expenditure, advertising etc. assuming itself to be the mgt. group of a simulated or approximate firm.

(c) Role Playing

Its purpose is to increase the trainee's skill in dealing with other people. One of its greatest use in connection with human relations training, but it is also used in sales training as well. It is spontaneous acting of a realistic situation involving two or more persons under class-room situations. It is a method of human interaction which involve, stage play or realistic behaviour in an imaginary or hypothetical situation. Participants are typically provided with a specific situation which they must analyse, and then each participant assumes and acts out the role of a specific person. Role-playing has many advantages. By this method, a trainee can broaden his experience by trying different approaches, while in actual situation, he often has only one chance.

(d) Films and TV Shows

These are also useful technique for training. It is an effective techniques of transmitting information and of enriching the knowledge of trainees. They generate interest among trainees by dramatising these usually specific events, incidents and realities. These technique can be used by other approaches like lectures and conferences to brush up trainees.

The other teams assume themselves a competitors and react to the decision. This immediate feed-back helps to know the relative performance of each team.

(e) Case Studies or Case Discussions

A case is a written account of a trained reporter of analyst seeking to describe an actual situation. Some cases are merely illustrative, others are detailed and comprehensive demanding extensive and intensive analytical ability. Cases are widely used in a variety of programmes. Cases are prepared on the basis of actual experiences of organisations, i.e., actual business situations that happened in various organisations. Case studies involve providing the trainees with written or video taped descriptions of *decision making situations* or cases. The participants are required to analyse each case and make appropriate decisions.

(f) In Basket Exercise

The trainee is given background information about a simulated company, its products, key personnel various memos, latters, request, *and all data pertaining* to the firm that a manager might find in the in basket upon arriving at work. The trainee has to understand all this make note, delegate tasks, and prepare memos within a specified amount of time. In basket exercise develops various kinds of abilition in the trainee such as - (i) situational judgement in being able to recall details, establish prioritic, interrelate items, and determine need for more information, (ii) Willingness to make decision and take action, (iii) Good time mgt. which is important enough in most managerial jobs.

(g) 360 Degree Feed-Back

The idea of upward feed-back developed by firms are called 360 Degree of Feed-Back. In this an employee's performance information is collected "all round" that is from his supervisors, subordinates, peers and internal or external customers. This feed-back is very useful for training and development. The computerized system compile or collect all this feed-back information and facts into individualized reports that are prepared and presented to the person being rated, which becomes useful for the ratees to meet their own supervisors and sometimes with their subordinates to share the information what they deserve is essential for the purpose of skill building.

(2) *Behaviourally Anchored Rating Scale (BARS)* : It is designed to identify the job's critical areas of performance and to describe behaviour of the job which is more effective and less effective for getting results. Performance is evaluated by asking the rater to record specific and observable job behaviour of an employee and then to compare these observations with a "behaviourally anchored rating scale". As a result the supervisor is in a position to compare the employee's actual behaviour with behaviour that has been previously determined to more or less effective.

BARS method has several advantages. First, the ratings are likely to be accurate because these are done by experts. Secondly, the method is more reliable and valid as it is job specific and identifies observable and measurable behaviour. The rater's bias is reduced. Systematic clustering of critical incidents helps in making the dimensions independent of one another. Thirdly, ratings are likely to be more acceptable due to employee participation.

BARS method, has several disadvantages: First, it is very time consuming and expensive to develop BARS for every job. Secondly, behaviors used are more activity-oriented than results-oriented.

(3) *Appraisal by Results (MBO)* : Result oriented appraisal is the outcome of the modern management technique known as management by objective (MBO). MBO has been described as a philosophy of management which seeks to minimize external controls and maximize internal motivation through joint goal setting between the manager and the subordinate and increasing the subordinate's own control of his work. 'Management by objectives can be described as a process whereby the superior and subordinate managers of an organisation jointly identify its common goals, define each individuals major areas of responsibility in terms of results expected of him and use these measures as guides for operating the unit and assessing the contribution of each of its members.

These are the engaging steps in performance evaluation through which MBO are to be listed in quick succession.

(1) *Set Organisation objectives* : First, all objectives of the organisation conspicuous as of performance are laid down. The objectives are to be defined in lucid, precise and measurable terms. They should be challenging yet approachable. An in depth evaluation of internal environment and external environment of the organisation is made to set these objectives.

(2) *Defining process targets* : On the score of organizational goals performance norms for each and every employee may be decided on the ground of organisation charts and job description. Every subordinate write down his own performance objectives which are coupled with work and job orientation. His manager also writes down the goals he thinks the subordinate should strive for. The two then embark upon the discussion reach an agreement and put the agreed goals in writing. Thus, employees are dynamically engrossed in goal setting. Clear attainable goals help canalize energies in the healthy direction. And the employees should be acquainted with the basis on which he would be appraised. These goals are periodically revived and revived to keep them flexible and updated.

The level of performance is satisfactory enough to notch up the goal defined lucidly and clearly. Measure check point are established to fathom progress towards the goals. Action plans needed to attain the goals are decided through mutual consultation among the employee and his superior. Joint goal setting and joint action planning are the important ingredients of appraisal through MBO.

(3) *Performance reviews :* Recurrent performance meetings between the manager and the subordinate should be held. Monthly review may be used and then extended to quarterly reviews. In the review meetings, there is an assessment of weakness and constraints identified and step to be initiated to streamline the performance to be decided. Subordinate take part in the process in an active manner. This paves way to self-control by the employee.

(4) *Evaluation :* After every performance review, feedback or performance is conveyed to the employee so that he could regulate and improve on his own performance on the score of performance. Review rewards are also decided. Novel goals and performance targets are decided for the next period.

Test Questions

1. Distinguish between performance appraisal and potential evaluation through modern methods.
2. Describe the process of performance appraisal through modern methods.
3. How can performance appraisal be made more effective? Discuss.
4. Explain the essentials of an effective performance appraisal system.
5. Write notes on -
   a) Assessment Centre.
   b) Behaviorally Anchored Rating Scales.
   c) Appraisal by Results or MBOs.

9

Job Evaluation

Job evaluation is the result of job analysis. Job analysis provides information about jobs, which is necessary for compensational specialists to begin the next phase of compensation management job evaluation.

The most difficult and the important function of personnel management is to fix the wage rate for each job in the organisation and it is not possible unless the relative worth of jobs is known. In order to determine the relative worth of the job in comparison to other jobs in the organisation, job evaluation is the most current and systematic technique. In other words it is a formal system of determining base compensation of jobs. The main objective of this technique is to ascertain the relative worth of the job through an objective evaluation so that relative compensation may be fixed for each job.

"Job evaluation represents an effort to determine the relative value of every job in a plant and to determine what the fair basic wage for such a job should be."

In brief, job evaluation seeks to rank all jobs in the organisation and place them in a hierarchy that will reflect the relative worth of each. Remarkably, this is a ranking of jobs an people.

Objectives of Job Evaluation

(1) to determine the hierarchy of job.

(2) to minimise wage discrimination on the basis of age, sex, caste, region, religion, etc.

(3) to compare the duties, responsibilities and demands of a job with that of other job.

(4) to develop a consistent wage policy.

(5) to eliminate wage inequities

(6) to gather data and information relating to job description, job specification and employee specifications of various jobs in an organisation.

(7) to provide a basis for wage negotiations with trade unions.

(8) to provide a framework for periodic review and revision of wage rates.

(9) to determine equitable wage differentials between different jobs in the organisation.

Process of Job Evaluation

1.Formation of a Job Evaluation Committee. It is very difficult for a single person to evaluate all jobs objectively. Therefore, a committee consisting of *experienced and respected representatives of management and workers and outside experts* should be constituted. Participation of employees in job evaluation will reduce their doubts and suspicion about the programme.

2. Job Analysis. Job analysis is the prerequisite for job evaluation. All necessary informations are collected through it. It defines the activities involved, job requirements, machines, tools and materials to be used, time taken by the employees in completing a given task and abilities of employees to meet the job evaluation.

3. Job Description. In job description the information collected by the job analysis process is systematically presented in a prescribed form for each job in the organisation. It defines the title of the job; analyses the job into its constituent tasks and record why, how and when these are done; states the responsibilities involved and conditions of employment for each job. This information is very important for evaluating the job.

4. Evaluation and Classification of Job. A job is compared with other jobs in terms of significant factors which may be as follows. Skill, mental and manual, experience, efforts and initiative, working condition, responsibilities to be undertaken, supervision required. Evaluation meetings should be conducted to review the Manual and evaluation factors.

5. Periodic Review. Job evaluation programme should be periodically reviewed and revised in order to keep them uptodate in the light of technological, economic and other changes so that they do not fail in view of the changed job situations. For this purpose a permanent job evaluation committee should be established to *review annually all the job descriptions and to conduct quarterly* meetings to review old jobs as well as newly created jobs. Even the most technically perfect plan can't survive if proper care is not taken to maintain its use.

Advantages of Job Evaluation

1. Job evaluation is a logical and objective technique of ranking jobs and thereby removing wage inequities. It is helpful in developing an equitable, rational and consistent wage and salary structure.
2. It helps to improve industrial relation by reducing employee doubts and grievances arising out of wages.
3. It helps in fitting new jobs at their appropriate places in the existing wage structure.
4. It simplifies wage administration by making wage rates more uniform.
5. It facilitates job redesign by re-allocating the easy and difficult tasks equally among different jobs.

Limitation of Job Evaluation

1. Since it takes a long time to instal and is quite costly, a system of job evaluation is rather difficult to introduce in smaller concerns.
2. Job evaluation is not fully objective and scientific. There is no standard list of factors to be considered and some job factors can't be measured.

3. Nature of jobs differ though they are allotted in the same grades.
4. It makes the wage and salary structure inflexible by freezing wage differentials between jobs.
5. Unrealistic because labour market conditions are ignored.
6. It is not well suited for determining the relative worth of managerial jobs.
7. Job evaluation is a time-consuming and expensive process and some methods are difficult to understand.
8. Limitations of evaluators also affect the technique.

Essentials for the Success of Job Evaluation Programme

1. The focus should be on rating the job and not the job holder. Each element should be rated on the basis of what the job itself requires.
2. The techniques used should be simple to understand for the employees.
3. Clear and accurate job descriptions should be prepared and jobs should be standardised before starting the evaluation process.
4. Too many occupational wages should not be established.
5. For the job evaluation programme support of top management must be won.
6. All the employees should be provided with complete information.
7. The acceptance and support of the trade unions should be obtained.

Methods of Job Evaluation

Various methods of job evaluation may be grouped as under -

1. Non-quantitative methods

   a. Ranking or job comparison.

   b. Grading or job classification.

2. Quantitative Methods

a. Point rating.

b. Factor comparison.

1. Non-Quantitative Method

(a) *Ranking Method* : In this method, each job as a whole is compared with other job. After comparison, all jobs are arranged from the highest to the lowest in order of their importance as judged by duties, responsibilities and demands on the job holder.

Advantages of Ranking Method

(i) It is very economical and less time is taken in evaluating the job.

(ii) The system is quite simple and easy. An organisation does not experience any difficulty installing this method.

(iii) Ranking system is suitable for smaller organisation where the raters are fully acquainted with all the existing jobs in the enterprise.

Disadvantages of Ranking Method

(i) If a new job is to be introduced in the organisation it becomes a matter of dispute which rank should be allotted to it.

(ii) There is no scientific approach in determining the rank of the job.

(iii) The system decides the ranks of the jobs on the basis of their importance but does not tell the reasons.

(b) *Job Classification or Grading Method :* It involves the establishment of job classes or grades. It was evolved as an improvement over the ranking method. Job descriptions and job specifications are widely used on it. The committee of executives goes through each job description and carefully weights it in the light of certain factors like skills, responsibilities, experience and type of work, etc. Thus, each job is assigned grade or class and for each.

Advantages

1. This method is easy to understand and simple to operate.

2. It is more accurate and systematic than the ranking method.
3. It is economical and therefore suitable for small concerns.

Disavantages

1. It is very difficult to write accurate and precise description.
2. It is difficult to classify such jobs in a particular grade.
3. The system is rigid and personal judgement is involved in deciding job classes and assigning jobs to specific classes.

2. QUANTITATIVE METHOD

Factor-comparison Method : This method is a combination of the ranking and point systems. All jobs are compared to each other for the purpose of determining their relative importance by selecting four or five major job elements or factors which are more or less common to all jobs. These elements are not predetermined. These are chosen on the basis of job analysis. The five factors which are customarily used are - (i) mental requirements, (ii) skill, (iii) physical requirements, (iv) responsibilities and (v) working conditions. The number of factors may be more than five.

Procedure Involved Are

(i) Various factors as given above are selected and defined clearly.
(ii) Key jobs are selected.
(iii) Wages are fixed for different factors of each key job.
(iv) A comparison scale is developed. Each key job is fitted to it. When all the key jobs have been evaluated and wages allocated in this manner, a job comparison scale is constructed.
(v) Jobs are evaluated factor, in relation to key jobs on job comparison scale. Then each jobs is to be evaluated and compared to other jobs in terms of each factor, and
(vi) A wage structure is designed, adjusted and operated.

Advantages Of Factor Comparison Method

(i) It is flexible as it has no upper limit on rating that a job may receive on a factor.

(ii) It utilizes few factors and thereby reduces the likelihood or overlapping.

(iii) The system results in more accurats job evaluation as it is more objective because weights are not selected arbitary.

(iv) The procedure of rating new jobs by comparing with other standards or key job is logical and not too difficult to accomplish.

Disadvantages of Factor Comparison Method

(i) It is very difficult to allot due weightage to each factor.

(ii) Job evaluation under this system is made by experts. The programme cannot be developed by the management independently, without the help of specialists.

(iii) The contents and the value of these jobs may change over a period of time and this will lead to future errors.

(iv) It is costly to install and somewhat difficult for anyone who is not acquainted with the general nature of job evaluation technique to grasp.

Point Method

It is the most widely used method of job evaluation. Under this, jobs are divided into component factors. These factors are: skill, responsibility, effort and working conditions. Point or weights are assigned to each factor depending on the degree of its importance in a particular job. The total points for a job indicate its relative worth or value.

Advantages of Point Method

1. This system is most suitable for large enterprises.
2. This method is more effective because the major factors are sub-divided which ensures accuracy of evaluation.

Disadvantages of Point Method

1. The award of point values results in developing a ceiling and floor for each job.
2. It is difficult to apply this method to managerial jobs wherein the work content is not measurable in quantitative terms.

Test Questions

1. Define Job Evaluation. How does it differ from analysis and potential evaluation?
2. Explain the procedure involved in the evaluation of a job.
3. "Job evaluation determines the worth of a job and not of job holder". Comment.
4. Explain nonquantitative methods of job evaluation. What are the weaknesses of these methods?
5. How can a job evaluation programme be made more effective?

10
Wage Determination

Wages and salaries represent a substantial part of total costs in most of the organisations. Though for the economists these are variable cost, but for the businessmen, they are becoming ever increasing costs in view of the ability of unions to win upward adjustments. Wage and Salary Administration is one of the most important areas of human resource management. Every human resource manager is entrusted with the responsibility of establishing an equitable Wage and Salary Structure on one hand and maintaining an equitable labour cost structure on the other. Wage and Salaries represent a substantial part of total costs in most of the organisation. Human resource manager of present age is surrounded between the conflicting interests of the employees and the employers. Still for the successful functioning of the organisation Wage and Salary Administration is essential.

Wage and Salaries are sometimes considered synonimous but they have slightly diff meanings. Wages are paid on daily basis or even hourly basis and is used most frequently for products and maintenance of employee, generally known as "blue-collar workers." While salaries are paid on monthly basis who provide mental labour to the employer such as clerical, professional sales and management employees generally known as white collar workers.

What are the Determining Factors for the Wages of Workers?

(1) The determining factors for the wages of workers are important not only from the organisational angle of vision but from employee's point of view too. It is important from the organisational point of view because wages stake claim for the largest chunk of total cost of production and a plethora of other pressing problems such as production capacity, efficiency of labour, selling price, profits and industrial relations dependent upon wages. And it is important from employee's point of view because the provision of minimum wage as furnished by law. Secondly, the fair wage should also be taken into consideration account, certain minimum need of a family for food, fuel, clothing better and social requirements such as health and education so that management should pay attention to the problems by giving proper care and attention in systematic, scientific as well as phychologically to have a substantial truth.

Essentials of Sound Wage and Salary Administration

The following requirement must be fulfilled:

1. *Simplicity* : A good wage plan is one which is easy to understand and simple to operate. An average worker must be able to know the incentives offered and what he is expected to do. The monetary benefits must be made clear to all workers. This will create initiative and interest among them.

2. *Motivation* : A good wage plan should be provide an incentive to workers to produce more. This can be done by linking wages with output. Workers should be given a share in the gains of higher productivity. Initiative and sound judgement should be rewarded.

3. *Definiteness* : An incentive plan must be definite. This means frequent changes should not be made as such changes create confusion and doubts in the minds of workers. Such plan must give clear benefits to workers.

4. *Flexibility* : The wage plan must be capable of being adjusted quickly to the changing requirements of the enterprise. It should permit an early detection and correction of mistakes.

5. *Wide Coverage* : An incentive plan should not be for employees of certain sections only. It should have wide coverage and almost all the employees should be covered by such plan. Such wide coverage makes the plan popular at all levels and among all categories of workers.

6. ***Stability*** : The system of wage payment should be permanent and stable. Fluctuating system may create a doubt in the mind of workers. Changes in the wage plan should not be made unless there is a substantial change in the methods of work.

7. ***Result Oriented*** : The wage plan should establish a direct relationship between effort and reward. It would provide for higher wages to more efficient workers.

8. ***Workers' Participation*** : Wage incentive plan is installed primarily to benefit the persons who will in any way be affected by its installation. So the management must discuss the wage incentive system with the employees and their representatives.

9. ***Mutual Co-operation*** : The wage system should promote co-operation between employer and workers. The wage plan should be installed with the co-operation and understanding of the workers.

10. ***Reasonable Standards*** : Standards of work used in a wage plan should be reasonable. They should be neither two easy nor too difficult to achieve. Too easy standards would increase the costs and there by defeat the very purpose of the incentive wage plan.

Factor Affecting Wages

1. ***Cost of Living*** : The cost of living of workers also has a strong influence on the rate of wages. If this factor is not considered, the labourer may not be in a position to manage their needs and this will affect their efficiency.

2. ***Demand for and Supply of Labour*** : Forces of demand for and supply of labour determine the going wage rate. When there is no shortage of labour (as in India) wages tend to be low. But if there is shortage of labour, the wages demanded by workers shall be high. On the other hand, executive salaries have increased in India, after liberalisation, due to rise in demand for professionally trained managers.

3. ***Ability to Pay*** : If the firm is marginal and can't offered to pay competitive rates to its employees will generally leave it for better paying jobs. Ability to pay is an important faith affecting wages, not only for the individual firm but also for the entire economy

or industry.

4. ***Labour Unions*** : Well organised labour union exert pressure for higher wages and allowances. This pressure is exercised through collective bargaining, strikes and other methods.

5. ***Prevailing Wage Rates*** : While fixing wages, prevailing wages in the particular industry/region are taken into account. This is necessary to attract and retain qualified workers.

6. ***Job Requirements*** : If a job requires higher skill, responsibility and risk, the worker placed on that job will naturally get higher wages in comparison to other jobs which do not require the same degree of skill, responsibility and risk.

7. ***Productivity*** : Productivity is the key factor in the operation of a company. High wages and low costs are possible only when higher wages are paid in firms, where productivity increases appreciably.

8. ***State Regulation*** : State regulation is another important factor for influencing wage rates, as the state assumes responsibility for safeguarding the interests of citizens. It has to step in to regulate the wage rates of labourers through legislative measures.

Methods Of Wage Payment

1. ***Time Wage-System*** : Under this system the worker is paid for the amount of time spent on the job irrespective of the amounts of work done. The period of time may be a day, a week, a fortnight or a month. When the unit of time is a day, such wages are popularly known as 'daily wage' basis and the workers who belong this are daily wagers, and the method is called Daily Wage System.

Merits of Time Wage System

(i) Simplicity is the greatest merit of the system. Workers can easily compute their own remuneration.

(ii) Earnings of workers are regular and fixed. Thus same amount of wages and same equality prevails.

(iii) The plan is economical as no detailed records of output are required.

(iv) As worker is not in a hurry to do his job to speed up production, the quality of work is maintained.

(v) This method also avoids wasteful handling of materials and tools.

Demerits

(i) The method provides no incentive for better performance because reward is not proportionate to effort and between the honest worker and the shirker.

(ii) Guaranteed remuneration makes workers indifferent and complacant.

(iii) As both a good and a bad workers are paid alike, the system suppresses good works as there is no incentive to hard work.

Suitability Under Following Conditions -

1. When it is difficult to fix the standard time for doing a job.
2. Where work is not repetitive and standardised.
3. Where quality rather than quantity of output is the basic target.
4. When delays in work are frequent and beyond the control of employees, i.e., where output is uncertain and irregular.

Piece Wage System

Under this system, remuneration is based on the amount of work done or the no. of units of goods turned out irrespective of the time. One units of output is considered as one piece and a specific rate of wage is paid per piece.

Merits

1. There is a direct relation between effort and reward.
2. Payment is based on results of efficiency hence this system recognises merit. Improve their standard of living and morale.
3. The method is just and fair to all.

4. The cost of supervision becomes comparatively less as the workers tend to drive themselves in their own interest.

Demerits

1. It is very difficult to fix piece wage rates because a worker may earn below the subsistence fevel due to breakdown of machinery or power, non availability of materials, etc.
2. The cost of supervision becomes comparatively less as the workers tend to drive themselves in their own interest.
3. To increase their earnings, workers work with high speed which is injurious for their health.

Suitability

1. When productivity of the workers is to be increased and output can be measured accurately, e.g., production of standardised goods in the factory.
2. When the quantity of output is more important than its quality.
3. Where the flow of worker is regular and interruptions are minimum, i.e., repetitive jobs.

Balance or Debt Method

This method is not separate rather a combination of time and piece wage system. The worker is guaranteed a time rate with an alternative piece rate. If the wages calculated at piece rate exceed the time rate, the worker get credit. On the other hand, if time wages exceed piece wages, the worker is paid time wage and the deficit is carried forward to be reconsidered in future.

This method provides security to employees. At the same time an employees is given the opportunity to increase his earnings beyond the guaranted time wage. This method is appropriate in industries where the flow of work is minimum, e.g., dock workers.

The Process Of Wage Determination

It consists of the following—

(i) *Job Analysis* : It is the process by which data in regard to each job is systematically observed and noted. It provides information about the nature of the job and the characteristics or qualifications that are desirable in the job holder. The job analysis study aims to provide information in these basic areas: like job description and job specification. Then on the basis of two items standards of job performance are laid down.

(ii) ***Job Evaluation*** : It is a systematic method of appraising the value of each job in relation to other jobs in the organisation.

(iii) ***Setting Wage Structure*** :The main concern should be to maintain adequate wage differentials between jobs at different levels in the organisational hierarchy. Determining such a structure several points need to be considered.

(iv) ***Guidelines for wage administration***

1. What the rules framed for the employees should be informed?
2. What extent salary advancement will be based on length of service and to what extent on merit?
3. What will be the rate for the enhancement of pay on the basis of performance of the employee?

(v) ***Potential Evaluation*** : The purpose of potential evaluation is to determine the reward or punishment that should be met out to an individual. Potential can only be judged with reference to targets or allotted tasks. The results can be assessed only in terms or predetermined objectives.

(vi) ***Wage Survey*** : The purpose of wage survey is to determine the extent to which the organisation pay scales are like those of other enterprises in the region. The wage and salary practices of other organisations have an important impact on the employment, retention and morale of the personnel. So they must be taken into consideration while fixing the wages for different jobs in an organisation.

Concepts of Wages

In our country three concepts of wages have evolved namely:

(i) Minimum Wage.

(ii) Fair Wage.

(iii) Living.

These are called basic wages.

Minimum Wage

A minimum wage may be defined as that wage which is sufficient to cover the bare physical needs of a worker and his family. A reasonable standard of living should be permitted to the worker from the stand-point of this health, efficiency and well being. Statutory minimum wage is fixed from this point of view.

There is a distinction between a bare subsistence of minimum wage and a statutory minimum wage. The former is a wage which would be sufficient to cover the bare physical needs of a worker and his family. This is a wage which has got to be paid to the worker irrespective of the capacity or the industry to pay. If an industrial organisation is unable to pay to its workers at least a bare minimum, it has no right to exist.

Fair Wage

One of the most important slogan of labour is equal pay for equal work. It is the wage that received by employees performing equal work and demanding equal skills, equal difficulty and equal unpleasantness. Equal work is to be considered not only on the same job but also work in similar and comparable jobs. Fair wage is the predominant rate available for similar job and occupation throughout the country.

Living Wage

According to the Fair Wage Committee Report, "The living wage should enable the male earner to provide for himself and his family not merely the bare essentials of food, clothing and shelter, but also a measure of frugal comfort including education for children, protection against ill health, requirements of essential social needs and a measure of insurance against the more important misfortunes including old age." Thus, practically, living wage is a wage which provide the workers with a standard of life furnishing him the necessities of life plus certain amenities considered necessary for the well being of the worker determined in terms of the position of the worker in a particular society. The Fair Wages Committee was of the opinion that minimum wages must be given to the workers and living wage should be target.

According to the Fair Wage Committee, the goal of living wage should be achieved in three stages. In the first stage, the payment of wage to the entire working class should be established and stabilised. In the second stage, fair wages should be established in the community and industry. In the third stage, the working class should be paid the living wage. The living wage may be somewhere between the lowest limit of the minimum wage and the highest limit of the living wage, depending upon the bargaining power of the labour.

In India a few more wage packages are available like Dearness Allowance, Bonus and Fringe Benefits. Now let us have a glimpoe over it.

Dearness Allowance (D.A.)

Under Section-3 of the Minimum Wages Act it is described as cost of living allowance. This allowance is given to protect the real wages of workers during inflation.

Bonus

It is a share of workers in the prosperity of an enterprise, it may also be regarded as an incentive to higher productivity.

Fringe Benefits

It is an indirect financial aid to the employee sometimes measurable in money and some times not. It is given to the employees during and post employment period which are connected with the employment but not the employees contribution to the organisation. These benefits suppliments to the workers ordinary wages.

Test Questions

1. Explain the principles of wage and salary administration.
2. What do you understand by wage and salary administration?

   Disus the essentials of a sound wage and salary structure.

3. Why wages of workers be determined?
4. Differentiate between Minimum Wage, Fair Wage and Living Wage.
5. What are the principal methods of wage payments? Examine their relative merits and demerits.
6. What are the objectives of wage and salary administration? What factors should be considered in fixing wages?

11
Industrial Relations and Trade Unions

The industrial relations are a product of the interaction between the social, political and economic system though they are not the cause but effect of the social, political and economic forces. The relationship between employers and employees or Trade Unions is called Industrial Relations.

Industrial Relations

Industrial relations deal with the nature of working relationship that subsists between the two partners in production, management and workers. One thing is clear that if the relationship is good, and management and workers work in a spirit of goodwill and understanding, production will be maximised. On the other hand if the relationship is one of friction and lack of goodwill, workers will not be at their best. Production will suffer, and losses will be inevitable. Production, as said earlier, is a social function and so long as a production unit exists it is to the interest of all that it functions at its best. But whether, we can acknowledge that this would happen as a self-motivating process. If not why not-and in that case, what are the remedies? These are deep-rooted problems which touch our social fabric at many points—legal, economic and political.

But within the framework of the organisation, there may be

new organised pattern. And one such pattern—the most potent, powerful and capable of changing the social face and surface is the rise of trade unionism.

Significance of Industrial Relation

Healthy industrial relation helps the organisation in the following ways -

(a) *Industrial Peace* : Cordial industrial relations bring harmony and remove causes of disputes. This leads to industrial peace which is an ideal situation on the industrial front.

(b) *Conducive environment for new programmes* : New programmes for workers development are introduced in the atmosphere of peace such as training facilities, labour welfare facilities, etc. It increases the efficiency of workers resulting in higher and better production at lower costs.

(c) *High employee morale* : Good industrial relations improve the morale of the employees. Employees work with greater zeal with the feeling in mind that the interest of employers and employee is one and the same, i.e., to increase production, every worker feels that he is a co-owner of the industry. The employer in his turn must realize that the gains of industry are not for him done but they should be shared equally and generously with his workers.

(d) *Fair benefits to workers* : The workers should get sufficient economic and non-economic benefits to lead a happy life. It is possible when the relations between the workers and management and smooth and the productivity is high. The employers can afford higher benefits to the workers.

(e) *Reduces Industrial disputes* : Good industrial relations reduce the industrial disputes. Disputes are reflection of the failure of basic human urges or motivations. Adequate satisfaction or expression are fully cured by good industrial relations. Strikes, lockouts, go slow tactics, gherao and grievances are some of the selection of industrial unrest which do not spring up to an atmosphere of industrial peace. It helps promoting co-operation and increasing production.

(f) *Reduce wastage* : Good industrial relations are maintained on the basis of co-operation and recognition of each other. It will help to increase production. Wastages of man, material and machines are reduced to the minimum and thus national interest is protected.

Thus, good industrial relations is the basis of higher production with minimum cost and higher profits. It also results in increased efficiency of workers. Now and new projects are introduced for the welfare of the workers and to promote the morale of the people at work.

Causes of Poor Industrial Relations

Economic, Educational, Cultural, Technological and Political Factors are responsible for poor industrial relations.

(1) *Economic Cause* : Wages should be considered as need based, taking into account certain minimum need of a family for food, fuel, clothing, shelter and social needs like - health and education. Otherwise poor wage will result into unhealthy relations among management and labour.

(2) *Educational Causes* : We known that industrial workers in India are generally illiterate and are misued by outside leaders. Education will be the only source which will bring a sense of commitment and responsibility in their behaviour. Lack of education has made them irresponsible.

(3) *Cultural Causes* : Culture affects the functioning of the organisation. Every organisation develops its own norms and cultural pattern of behaviour which is imposed on every worker. But sometimes workers go beyond this which results into growing intolerance, tensions and conflicts in organisation as well as in their families, breaking up of office union, family union even and leading to poor industrial relation.

(4) *Political Causes* : Political nature of trade unions, multiple unions and inter-union rivalry weaker trade union movement. In the absence of strong and responsible trade unions, collective bargaining becomes the effective. The political workers misue the industrial workers to serve the political purpose and arrange strikes, gherao, etc.

(5) *Technological Causes* : Technologies are fast work suffer and the costs rise. There is changing need for trained and skilled workers to handle those advanced machines. Workers go on strike off and on to resist rationalisation and automisation in industries.

Suggestions to Improve Industrial Relations

(1) *Sound Personal Policies* : All policies and rules relating to industrial relations should be clear to everybody in the enterprises to union leaders. It can be successful only when they are followed from top to bottom.

(2) *Cordial Attitude* : Both management and trade unions should have positive attitude towards each other. Management must recognise union as the spokesmen of worker's grievances and as custodians of their interests. The management should accept workers as equal partner's in a joint endeavour similarly workers must also consider and appreciate the rights, authority and responsibility of management.

(3) *Sound Personnel Qualities* : The entire industrial relation staff like—jobbers, foremen, supervisor etc. should be well trained and awarded in the tools, techniques, customs and practices and the framework of human relations as these are the people who come in direct touch of the employees. Hence they should be trained in leadership and communication practices well since a dynamic leadership may make the followers loyal to the organisation so that they may work hard towards the common goal. Similarly if the communication power is strong the personnel executive can get things done only through other people. He must learn not only to get acceptance of his ideas but also how to get in willing enthusiastic co-operation that results in benefits to all concerned with the work team and its production.

(4) *Management Aid* : Since industrial relations is a functional staff service, it must necessarily drive its authority from the line organisation. The goal of peaceful industrial relations could be cherished by the top management and personnel director (responsible for maintaining industrial relations) should support to a top line authority, say, president or chairman of the company.

TRADE UNION

Concept

It is a voluntary organisation of workers formed to protect and promote their interest through collective action. According to Giri they may be organised on plant, industry, firm on national basis.

Trade union in modern times is a phenomenon by itself. It is an association of workers formed to latter their living and working conditions. In India, under the Act of 1926, any seven members can apply for the formation of a trade union and get itself registered.

In other capitalist countries, the right to form trade union was given much earlier. Not that the right came as matter of gift from the above. The workers had to fight hard for it.

Trade unions are formed on the basis of three recognised principles. First, the workers have a right to organise, second, the right to collective bargaining and third the right to strike. Besides these basic rights, the trade unions can within their limited funds and capabilities undertake welfare functions.

Each of these three principles states clearly. That right to organinse is based on the principle that a worker as an individual is unequally placed against his employers. He is one among many who seek job from masters who are few. He cannot bargain with one against another. The position of the employer is just the reverse. He can pick and choose and his bargaining power is much greater than that of the worker.

Right to collective bargaining is based on the principle that a worker is no longer a helpless individual, his position is strengthened by union and combination, and bargaining about his work and pay need not be from the position of weakness of individual, but of strength of an organised and collective union demand. Unionism raises the morale of the worker. He is assured of the strength of the union and cannot therefore be victimised as a hapless individual worker.

The third one - that is the right to strike is based on the principal that, if the union collectively presents a demand - whether it is a demand for higher wages, change in working conditions and if with the best of efforts - bargaining fails — then what is the alternative for the worker? Within peaceful means—the workers therefore have one way left-that is the right to strike. Strike is organised cessation of work with a view to get grievances redressed.

Nature and Characteristics

- A trade union may be association or combination of employees or employers or of independents workers.
- Membership of a trade union is voluntary, generally, there is no legal or other pressure to join a trade union and a person can join or leave the union on his willingness.
- It is a continuing or permanent rather than a temporary or casual combination.
- The union is essentially a co-operative labour marketing association. It is an association of workers who engaged to protect and promote their economic and other interests.

Objectives, Functions or Role of Trade Union

(a) To improve, working conditions by securing shorter working hours., better leave facilities, adequate social security.

(b) To protect the longer interest of society by assisting in the improvement of trade and industry.

(c) Industrial peace.

(d) Collective bargaining

(e) To secure for workers fair wages.

(f) To enlarge opportunities for promotion and training.

(g) To provide for educational, cultural and recreational facilities.

(h) Installing in their members a sense of responsibility toward industry and community.

(i) Trade union are also expected to fulfil certain social responsibilities like promotion of national integration.

(j) Generally influencing the socio-economic policies of community through active participation in their formulation at various levels.

Structure of Unions

The structure of unions refer to the basis on which unions are organised (i.e., whether they are organised on craft or industrial or general union basis) and to the pattern whereby the plant unions are linked to regional level or national level federation or unions. Let us examine these two aspects one by one.

Trade unions can be classified into three categories: (a) Craft unions, (b) Industrial unions, and (c) General unions. A craft union is an organisation of wage earners engaged in a single occupation. It may cover all workers engaged in a particular craft irrespective of the industries in which they are employed. Thus, electricians though working in different industries, may from a union of electricians. Similarly, there may be separate unions for fitters, burners, carpenters, etc. The International Wood Carvers 'Association and the Indian Pilots' Guild may be cited as examples of craft unions.

An Industrial union is organised on the basis of an industry rather than a craft. Say, if the work force of a cotton textile factory decide to form a union consisting of workers of different industry the union will be called an industrial union. A general union is one whose membership covers workers employed in different industries and crafts. General unions are not popular in India.

In India, trade unions have largely been organised by industry rather than craft. Although industrial unions have grown continuously, craft unions have also emerged here and there. They exist among non-manual workers like administrative staff, professionals, technicians, etc.

Registration of Trade Unions

Under the Trade Unions Act 1926 only seven or more members of a trade union by subscribing their names to the rules of the trade union and otherwise complying with the provisions of this Act can apply for registration. The application has to be made to the Registrar of Trade Unions. This application must be accompanied by a copy of the rules of the trade union and a statement of the following particulars.

(1) the names, occupations and address of the members, making the application.

(2) the name of the trade union and the address of its head office and

(3) the names, ages, occupations, titles and address of the office bearers of the trade union.

Cancellation of Registration

A certificate of a trade union may be withdrawn or cancelled by the Registrar-

(a) On the application of the trade union to be verified in the prescribed manner.

(b) If the Registrar is satisfied that the certificate has been obtained by fraud or -

(c) If the Registrar is satisfied that the trade union has (i) ceased to exist (ii) wilfully discontinued any provisions of the act, or (iii) allowed any rule to continue in force, which is inconsistent with any such provision or (iv) rescinded any rule which ought to be there.

In case (b) & (c) the registrar has to give to the trade union not less than 2 months previous notice in writing specifying the ground on which it is proposed to withdraw or cancel the certificate of registration. No such notice is necessary in case (a).

Obstacles to the Development of Trade Union in India

(1) Uneven Growth. Trade Union are concentrated in large scale in the industry sector and also in big industrial centres. There is very little trade union activity in small sector, agricultural labour and domestic sector. Many workers still regard their employer as their 'mai-bap' and do not join unions.

(2) Small Size. Most of the unions have low membership, 80% of the unions are of less than 500 members. Any seven workers can form a union under the Trade Union Act 1926 and get it registered.

(3) Financial Crunch. The organisational yearly income of various unions is very low and inadequate. Due to their financial weaknesses, most of the unions are not in a position to undertake welfare programmes for workers.

(4) Outside Leadership. In India trade unions are in the hands of outsiders whose interests are not always identical with those of the workers. Such outsiders are generally professional men such as lawyers or social and political workers.

(5) Registration. The commission recommended that registration shall be cancelled if membership falls below the minimum limit or the union fails to submit the return in a proper way.

(6) Apathy of Members. Majority of workers do not take keen interest in union activities.

Measures for Strengthening of Trade Unions

(1) Development of Strong base. In order to develop a strong trade union movement it is essential to wider the unionism to unorganised sector and small towns. The membership of union should also be increased. For this purpose, a rigorous membership campaign should be launched.

(2) One Union one Industry. The principal of one union in one industry should be adopted to avoid multiple unions and inter-union rivalry.

(3) Development of Internal Leadership. Leaders of union should be developed from within the rank and file of the workers. This will help to gain strength. The National Commission on Labour recommended that - (1) hire should be no ban on non-members holding executive position in a union but (2) the limit of outsiders in the executives of the unions should not exceed 25% (3) ex-employees should not be treated as outsiders. (4) steps should be taken to promote internal leadership and give it more responsible role.

(4) Strengthening of Trade Union. The following step may be recommended -

(i) Small trade unions must be amalgamated into one big trade union who can organise the labour welfare activities well.

(ii) Improvement in the finances of trade unions should be made from internal resources. Membership fee may be enhanced and defaulters should not be allowed to continue their membership.

(iii) Attitude of employees needs change.

(5) Responsibility of Workers. At present trade unions confine their own attention to the workers demand only. They should first make every worker understand their duties and responsibilities and then their rights and privileges.

Test Questions

1. What do you understand by the term industrial relations? Explain the significance of industrial relations.
2. Discuss the main approaches to the study of industrial relations.
3. What is a trade union? Explain the objectives and functions of trade unions.
4. Distinguish between craft unions, industrial unions and central unions.
5. Define a trade union. Why do workers join unions?
6. Explain the procedure for registration of trade unions. What are the rights and liabilities of a registered union?
7. "Trade union movement in India has not developed on healthy lines". Discuss.
8. What are the weaknesses of trade union in India? Suggest measures to improve trade union movement in the country.

12

Dispute Resolution and Grievance Management

Meaning of Industrial Dispute

Industrial disputes are organised protests against existing terms and conditions of employment, dispute is a different kind of situation. It is a presparation for a show-down—a near collape in relationship. And if strikes or lockouts actually take place, the points of dispute remain unresolved—it means virtual breakdown. To deal with such a situation the appropriate law is the Industrial Dispute Act. But the Act, as said earlier, is curative and not preventive of disputes—that is it comes into operation only when disputes occur, but by itself, except perhaps in an indirect way, cannot prevent dispute and promote industrial peace and harmony.

According to section 2 of the Industrial Dispute Act, 1947, "Industrial Dispute means any dispute or difference between employers and employees or between employers and workmen or between workmen and worker, which is connected with the employment or non-employment or terms of employment or with the conditions of labour of any persons."

The Industrial Dispute is unrest in labour which expresses itself in many ways and forms. The most striking feature of the labour unrest expressed itself in the form of strikes or stoppage of work. As a result of strike the factories are closed down and this proves harmful both to employees and employers. Besides strikes, the unrest among labour may manifest itself in demonstrations, taking out processions, gherao, picketing, bikout, enlisting support of politician, etc.

Methods For The Prevention And Settlement Of Industrial Dispute

(a) Methods for Prevention

(1) Worker's Participation in Management

It is a method whereby the workers are allowed to be consulted to have a say in the management of the unit. The important scheme of worker's participation are: Works Committee, Joint Management Council (JMC), Shop Council and Joint Council, Now we have a brief idea about the above committee and council.

(i) **Works Committee :** In the case of any industrial establishment in which 100 or more workers are employed, a work committee consisting of employers and workers is to be established. The committee will have equal number of representation. It shall be the duty of the works committee to promote measures for securing and preserving amity and good relations among the workers and their employers, to comment up a matter of their common interest and to compose any material difference of opinion in respect of such matters.

(ii) **Joint Management Councils :** These consist of equal representatives of employers and workers, not exceeding twelve, at the plant level in selected industrial establishment. In case of any industrial establishment who employs at least five hundred workers, should have a well established and strong central organisation of employees' unions and should have a record to good industrial relations. A joint management council has been provided under the workers participation in Management scheme. This scheme also consider the matters of common interest like:

(a) The council is to be consulted by management before introducing any changes in the modes of production, production schedule, general administration problem, etc.

(b) The council is to receive information, discuss and give suggestions on general economic situation, state of the market, production and marketing programmes, organisation and general functioning of the concern, methods of production and work, balance sheet and profit and loss account, long term capital budgeting decisions, plans for expansion, modernisation and development, etc.

(c) The council is entrusted with the responsibility of administering welfare measures, supervision of safety and health schemes, vocational training, apprenticeship schemes, scheduling of working hours, breaks and holidays and reward for suggestions.

(iii) **Shop Councils :** There shall be a shop council for each department or shop whether a joint management council already exists or not.

Each shop council shall consist of equal number of representatives of employers and workers. The employers' representatives shall be nominated by the management and must consist of persons from the unit concerned.

The number of members of each council may be determined by the employer in consultation with the recognised union in the manner that best suited to local conditions obtaining in the unit. The total number of members may not generally exceed 12.

Shop councils were to deal with the following matters:

(a) Assist management in achieving production targets.

(b) Assist in maintaining general discipline in the shop/ department.

(c) Identify areas of low productivity and take necessary steps at shop level so as to eliminate the cause of low productivity.

(d) Suggest health, safety and welfare measures to be adopted for smooth functioning of the shop or department.

(e) Study absenteeism in the shop/department and recommend steps to reduce them.

(iv) **Joint Councils:** In every industrial establishment who employs

500 or more workers there was to be a joint council for the whole establishment. The main features of the scheme were as follows:

- A joint council shall function for a period of two years.
- Only such members who are actually engaged in the unit shall be members of the joint council.
- The chief executive of the unit shall be the Chairman of the joint council. There shall be a vice-chairman who will be nominated by worker-members of the council.
- The joint council shall appoint one of the members as its secretary. The joint council shall meet at least once in a quarter.
- A joint council was to deal with the following matters:
- Matters emanating from shop councils which remain unresolved.
- Optimum production, efficiency and fixation of productivity norms of men and machine for the unit as a whole.
- Work planning and achieving production targets.
- Preparing schedules of working hours and of holidays.
- Developing skill of workmen and adequate facilities for training.

Rewards for valuable and creative suggestions received from workers.

General health, welfare and safety measures for the plant or the unit.

(2) Tripatriate Bodies

There are a number of Tripatriate Bodies which operate at the Central and State levels. The Indian Labour Conference, Standing Labour Committee, Wage Boards and Industrial Committees operate at the Central Level and State Labour Advisory Board at the State Level. All these bodies play an important role in reaching at voluntary agreements on various labour matters.

Indian Labour Conference (ILC) and Standing Labour Committee (SLC) have been constituted to suggest ways and means to prevent disputes. The representatives of the workers and employers are nominated to these bodies by the Central Government in consultation with the All-India organisations of workers and employers.

The agenda for ILC/SLC meetings is settled by the Labour Ministry considering the suggestions sent to it by member organisation. These two bodies work with minimum procedural rules to facilitate free and fuller discussions among the members. The ILC meets once a year, whereas the SLC meets as and when necessary.

The functions of ILC are: (a) to promote uniformity in labour legislation: (b) to lay down procedure for the settlement of industrial disputes; and (c) to discuss the matters of all India importance in between employers and employees. The ILC advises the Government on any matter referred to it for advice, taking into account the suggestions made by the States and representatives of the organisation of workers and employers. The Standing Labour Committee's (SLC) main function is to consider and determine such questions as may be referred to it by the Plenary Conference or the Central Government to render advice, take to into account the suggestions made by various governments, workers and employers.

(3) Code of Discipline

Code of Discipline is a set of self-imposed mutually agreed voluntary principles of discipline and good relations between the management and the workers in industry. In India a Code of Discipline was approved by the 16th Indian Labour Conference held in 1958.

According to the National Commission on Labour, the Code in reality has been of limited use. When it was started, very favourable hopes were thought of it; but soon it started acquiring rust. The main reasons for the lapses on the part of the employers and employees to secure harmonious relations through the Code may be listed as below:

1. There was absence of self-imposed voluntary restraint on the part of the parties.
2. The worsening of economic situation which led to the erosion of real wages of the workers.
3. The rivalry among labour representatives.
4. Conflicts between the Code and the law.

5. The state of indiscipline in the body public, that is, the whole set-up is charged with indiscipline and the Code could not work.
6. The employers could not implement the Code in many respects for reasons beyond their control.

(4) Standing Orders

To prevent the emergence of industrial strife over the conditions of employment, one important measure is the Standing Orders. Under the Industrial Employment Standing Orders Act, 1946, it was made obligatory that Standing Orders should govern the conditions of employment. The Standing Orders should regulate the conditions of employment from the stage of entry to the organisation to the stage of exit from the organisation. Thus, they form a regulatory pattern for industrial relations. Since the Standing Order provides Do's and Dont's they act as a code of conduct for the employees during their working life within the organisation.

The Standing Orders refer to rules and regulations governing the conditions of employment of workers. These rules regulate the conditions of employment, discharge, grievances, misconduct, disciplinary action, etc. of the workmen employed in industrial undertakings. These issues are potential problems in industrial relations.

Methods for Settlement

(1) Conciliation

"Conciliation is a method of resolving the industrial conflict with the help of third party, who intervenes in the dispute situation upon a request by either or both the parties. It is a procedure in which the decision-making function remains the prerogative of the parties to the dispute, as in collective bargaining. According to ILO it is a process of rational and orderly discussion of differences between the parties to a dispute under the guidance of a conciliator.

Conciliation, thus, is a form of mediation. Mediation is the act of making active effort to bring two conflicting parties to compromise. Mediation, however, differs from conciliation in that whereas conciliator plays only a passive and indirect role, and the scope of his functions is provided under the law, the mediator takes active part and the scope of his activities are not subject to any statutory provisions.

Conciliation Officers

The appropriate government has been authorised to appoint one or more conciliation officers for meditation in and promoting the settlement of industrial disputes. And the conciliation officer is given the powers of a civil court, whereby he is authorised to call and witness the parties on oath. It should be remembered, that civil court cannot go beyond interpreting the laws, the conciliation officer can go behind the facts and make judgement which will be binding upon the parties.

Board of Conciliation

It consists of a Chairman and two or four other members. The Chairman is to be an independent person and other members are nominated in equal numbers by the parties to the dispute. Conciliation proceedings before a Board are similar to those that take place before the Conciliation Officer. Yet the Government has another option of referring the dispute to the Court of Inquiry instead of the Board of Conciliation.

Court of Enquiry

In case of the failure of the conciliation proceedings to settle a dispute, the government can appoint a Court of Inquiry to enquire into any matter connected with or relevant to industrial dispute. The court is expected to submit its report within six months.

Appraisal

The performance of conciliation machinery can not be said to be heartening. Only 25per cent of cases are annually handled. It means petty issues are taken up for conciliation. Besides a very large number of disputes are filed and then withdrawn later on by workers or union. Similarly, a large number of cases are rejected as untenable, not satisfying the legal provisions. This shows lack of understanding of legal provisions. Finally, a substantial number of cases remain pending.

(2) Voluntary Arbitration

Voluntary arbitration means that the disputing parties themselves refer the dispute on their own to an arbitrator. Voluntary arbitration became popular as a method of setting differences between workers and management with the advocacy of Mahatma Gandhi, who had applied it very successfully in the Textile industry of Ahmedabad. However, voluntary arbitration was lent legal identity only in 1956 when Industrial Disputes Act, 1947 was amended to include a provision relating to it.

The provision for voluntary arbitration was made because of the lengthy legal proceedings and formalities and resulting delays involved in adjudication. It may, however, be noted that arbitrator is not vested with any judicial powers. He derives his power to decide the dispute from the agreement that parties have made between themselves regarding the reference of dispute to the arbitrator. The arbitrator submits his award to the government. The government then publishes it within 30 days of such submission. Award becomes enforceable on the expiry of 30 days of its publication.

Appraisal

Regarding the performance of voluntary arbitration (as a method of resolving disputes) it can be said at the very outset that it has failed to make much progress. There exists general indifference among parties to use voluntary arbitration as a method of settling disputes. Hardly 2 to 3 per cent of the disputes not settled by conciliation are referred to voluntary arbitration. National Commission on Labour has identified following causes for the failure of voluntary arbitration :

(i) Lack of arbitrators who command the confidence of the parties to the disputes.

(ii) Law provides for no appeal against the award given by arbitrator.

(iii) Easy availability of adjudication on the failure of negotiation or conciliation.

(iv) The absence of simplified procedure to be followed in voluntary arbitration.

(v) Absence of recognised unions which command confidence of the majority of the workers.

(3) Adjudication : (Compulsory Arbitration)

Adjudication is the ultimate legal remedy for the settlement of industrial disputes. It means intervention of a legal authority appointed by the Government to make a settlement which is binding on the parties. Adjudication consists of settling disputes through the intervention by the third party appointed by the government.

A dispute can be referred to adjudication if both the employer and the recognised union agree to do so. A dispute can also be referred to adjudication (by the Government even) if there is no consent of the parties in which case it is called 'compulsory adjudication.' These are discussed below: The law provides the adjudication to be conducted by the Labour Court, Industrial Tribunal or National Tribunal.

A. Labour Courts : The Labour Courts deal with disputes relating to :

(a) The propriety or legality of an order passed by an employer under the Standing Orders.

(b) The application and interpretation of Standing Order.

(c) Discharge and dismissal of workmen and grant of relief to them.

(d) Withdrawal of any statutory concession or privilege.

(e) Illegality or otherwise of any strike or lockout.

(f) All matters not specified in the third scheduled of Industrial Disputes Act, 1947. (It deals with the jurisdiction of Industrial Tribunals).

B. Industrial Tribunals : The Industrial Tribunal will deal with the following matters.

1. Wages including the period and mode of payment.
2. Compensatory and other allowances.
3. Hours of work and rest intervals.
4. Leave with wages and holidays.
5. Bonus, profit sharing, provident fund and gratuity.
6. Shift working otherwise than the accordance with the standing orders.
7. Rules of discipline.
8. Rationalisation.

9. Retrenchment.

10. Any other matter that may be prescribed.

(c) National Tribunals : These tribunals are meant for those disputes which, (as the name suggests) involved the questions of national importance or issues which are likely to affect the industrial establishments of more than one state.

It is worth noting that adjudication machinery has helped the workers to secure better benefits and better conditions of work. That is why, trade unions have preferred adjudication as an important instrument for higher wages, allowances, bonus and other benefits. Adjudication has also helped the workers in standardisation of these benefits and improving working conditions in the industrial establishments. It has protected the workers in several cases as the workers were not well-organised and had poor bargaining capacity.

However, the functioning of adjudication machinery has not been very satisfactory, particularly because of : (i) the delays involved, and (ii) the inefficient implementation of the awards.

The proceedings at adjudication take unduly long periods. About 50 to 60 percent of the cases are decided in more than a year. And 25per cent of the cases in between 6 to 12 months. Secondly, the state of the implementation of awards (requiring implementation) is also not very commendable : 30 to 40 per cent of the awards are not implemented by the date of enforcement. In 1976, this figure was as high as 77 per cent. Incomplete and abrupt implementation of awards create suspicion in the minds of workers and shake their faith in the machinery.

Some people also criticise adjudication because it has failed to achieve lasting industrial peace; it has prevented the growth of unions and has also prevented voluntary settlement of industrial disputes and growth of collective bargaining. In the words of V.V. Giri, "Where one party has lost and the other has won, the victor and the vanquished get back to their work in sullen and resentful mood towards each other, and neither can forget nor forgive The loser awaits the next opportunity to make good the loss, while the winner is carried away be a sense of victory which is not conducive to co-operation. Such an attitude of suppressed hostility in one party and an unconcealed satisfaction and triumph in the other may lead to transient truce but not lasting peace.

Grievance Management

In some cases, the employees have complaints against their employers while in others it is the employers who have a grievance against their employers. The grievances may be real or imaginary, valid or invalid, genuine or false. Broadly speaking, a complaint affecting one or more workers constitutes a grievance. The complaint may relate to the quantum of wages, the mode of payment for overtime work, leave interpretation of service conditions, working conditions, seniority fixation, promotion, transfer, work assignments, dismissal or discharge, bad food available in Canteen etc.

Grievance is a feeling of dissatisfaction among workers regarding anything concerned with their employment relationship.

According to Dale S. Beach, "grievance is any dissatisfaction or feeling or injustice in connection with one's employment situation that is brought to the attention of management.

Causes of Grievances

It may be classified like the following:

(1) Grievances Resulting out of Working Conditions

(i) Tight production standards.

(ii) Poor relationship with the Supervisor.

(iii) Non-availability of proper tools and machines.

(2) Grievance Resulting from Management Policy

(i) Wage rates

(ii) Overtime.

(iii) Seniority.

(iv) Transfer.

(v) Promotion.

(vi) Lack of career planning.

(vii) Leave.

(3) Grievance Resulting from Personnel Maladjustment

(i) Excessive self-esteem.

(ii) Over-ambition.

(iii) Impractical attitude to life.

(4) Grievance Arising from :llegal violation of

(i) Central or State Laws.

(ii) The collective bargaining agreement.

(iii) Company rules and regulations.

Desirable Features Pre-Requisites/Principles of Grievance Handling Procedure

The efficiency of grievance procedure depends upon the fulfilment of certain pre-requisites. These are -

(1) Clarity

(2) Promptness

(3) Conformity with prevailing legislation

(4) Simplicity

(5) Training

(6) Follow up/Periodic review

(7) Legal sanctity.

(1) Clarity. There should be clarity regarding each and every aspect of grievance procedure. An aggrieved employee must be informed about the person to whom a representation can be made, the form of submission (written or oral), the time limit for the redressal of grievance etc. Similarly, the redressing authority should be very clear about what is expected from him, what measures he can take, the limits within which he should resort to an action, etc.

(2) Promptness. Management should seek to resolve a grievance quickly after it has been submitted by the worker. Since justice delayed is justice denied, the procedure should aim at rapid disposal of the grievances.

(3) Conformity with prevailing legislation. While designing the grievance procedure, due consideration must be given to the existing statutory provisions.

(4) Simplicity. The grievance procedure should be simple. Every employee must understand different stages of the procedure, the forms to be filled up, the witnesses required, etc.

(5) Training. The success of the procedure also depends upon imparting training to the supervisors and union representatives in handling grievances.

(6) Follow up/Periodic review. The successful working of a grievance procedure depends upon a proper follow-up on the personnel department. The department should periodically review the procedure and introduce the essential structural changes making it more effective.

(7) Legal sanctity. The procedure should be in confirmity with the existing law. It should be designed to supplement the statutory provisions.

Factors to be Considered While Deciding Grievance Handling Procedure

Following factors should be considered by management while preparing the grievance handling procedure.

1. Grievance handling procedure should be amended from time to time according to the needs and requirements.
2. Grievances should be presented before the competent authority who may take a decision on the problem.
3. Size of grievance handling committee should be small.
4. Various levels of management should be determined for the principles of handling grievances.
5. The grievances must be settled at the earliest.

Settlement of Grievance/Grievance Handling Procedure in Indian Industry

Some important procedure tested and proved effective as suggested by Baer in his Book *Grievance Handling* are worth nothing:

1. Investigate and handle each and every case as though it may

eventually result in dispute.

2. Give employee a full hearing.
3. Enforce agreements in the true spirit and ensure unions identify specific contractual provisions allegedly violated..
4. Do not by action or inaction cause the employee or the union to default on their compliance with any contractual obligations.
5. Do not deny the grievance for reason of non-compliance.
6. Do not argue the merits the grievance first if the grievance is untimely.
7. Do not apply grievance remedy to an improper grievant.
8. Do not hold back the remedy if the organisation is wrong and apply the remedy to the persons wronged.
9. Do not assume a judicial or arbitral role.
10. Remember always that the union is a moving party.
11. Determine and ensure there has been equal treatment of employees.
12. Evaluate any political connotations of the grievance.
13. Do no practise Parkinson's Law in labour relations.
14. Permit reasonable lattitude to the unions in the manner of its presentation, but do not relinquish your authority.
15. Do not permit misconduct of union representatives.
16. Admit errors and take corrective action.
17. Use the grievance machinery as another channel of communication.
18. Demand proper productivity levels be maintained.
19. Control your emotions, remarks and behaviour.
20. Recognise employees as individuals. Do not fail to keep employees informed as to where they stand.

Grievance is like "headache". It is symptom and not a disease.

Diagnosed properly, treated appropriately and in time the organisation will be rid of the disease in the beginning itself.

Remember the cardinal principle "listening reduces the burden of the employees" and half the problem is already solved by listening. reduces the grief of the other party. "Patience, perseverance, a searching look from within, a wide look around and a long ahead" on the part of manager always ensure that the work of grievance handling machinery is reduced to a considerable and manageable extent.

The procedure of handling a grievance essentially varies from company to company, but the principles are practically the same. A grievance should be handled in the first instance at the lowest level, i.e., an employee will raise his grievance to his immediate superior. It may be a simple it is a grievance arising out of action of the same superior, the employee will first to him only.

The employee should be told of his line of appeal, if he does not get satisfaction from his immediate superior. Usually, the next higher authority is the departmental head. If he still remain dissatisfied, some procedures permit the employee to go to the personnel officer; or to bring in the union to speak on this behalf. The union should discuss the matter with the personnel officer. But in case no solution is found and a serious dispute is anticipated, the personnel officer will give a complete report to the higher management to whom the final appeal will go.

Justice delayed is justice denied, so action or grievances should be taken promptly before rumours spread and tempers rest. If a grievance is allowed to go beyond a reasonable time, it would have done lot of harm even if ultimately a solution is found and the grievance is redressed.

If a grievance is against an instruction given by a superior, in the interest of order and discipline, that instruction must be carried out; only then the employee can register his protest. Unless this procedure is carried out, it should be agreed that there will be no recourse to the official machinery of conciliation. There must also be no direct action from either side which might prejudice the case.

Test Questions

1. Why do industrial disputes arise? How can such disputes be settled?
2. Bring out the causes and consequences of industrial disputes. Discuss existing machinery for the settlement of industrial disputes in India.

   (Bangalore, 1977)
3. Define industrial dispute. What are the main causes of industrial disputes in India?
4. Make constructive suggestions for the minimisation and settlement of industrial disputes and for the establishment of better industrial relations in an industry.
5. Critically examine the institutional provisions for the resolution of industrial disputes within the legal framework in India.

   (Delhi, MBA, 1989)
6. Critically examine the legal framework for industrial dispute resolution in India. In what specific ways does the existing system inhibit collective bargaining? (Delhi, MBA, 1992)
7. Define grievance. Why do grievances arise?
8. Explain the procedure for redressal of grievances.
9. How can management know and understand employees grievances?
10. Explain the advantages of a grievance redressal procedure.
11. "A sound grievance procedure must contain some essential features". Explain.
12. How are grievances settled in Indian Industry?

13

Employee's Empowerment

This study relates with job satisfaction which is concerned with the attitude that certifies various aspects such as, supervision, pay, work itself, co-workers; promotion, etc. These components are weighted in making gratification to those social and psychological needs. For getting stimulation to the employees they require growth process, creativity and innovativeness to the large scale organization. To the large organization, jobs are structured and standardized. But the situation is still worse in the case of small scale organization because the workers are in the absence of job security and adequate work rewards. They find it extremely difficult to satisfy there basic physiological needs continually.

In general, many persons work today not because work offers any pleasure but there is no other way of earning a living. Increased employee alienation from the system of work is one of the important facets of work life these days. Under the circumstances, jobs do not seem to arouse interest nor satisfaction among the employees. ato the small organization, there is paucity of job satisfaction.

Literature concerned with job satisfaction. The job satisfaction is based on a three point scale to the organization. The three point scale has been preferred to the five point scale or the seven point scale keeping in mind the educational background, degree of technical knowledge possessed, the nature of the job handled by the employees in the small scale organization. But the most important advantage to the small scale organization is that there are followed various forms of benefits. For instance, close employer-employee relationships, face to face communication with employer and close interaction with co-workers.

But in the case of large scale organization there exists a high degree of specialization. Most of the jobs are graded, and employees are compartmentalized right from recruitment to recruitment. In such organizaton, jobs are also tried to a definite scheme of promotion in dealing with elaborated rules and regulations. More importantly, opportunities for career growth and advancement exist boosting employee's morale and satisfaction. But such rosy picture does not exist to the small scale organization. Expediency, in general, dictates the way in which daily operations are being processed. Employees do not always perform only one particular task and operations are always not time-bound.

In the large scale organization, there arise various factors such as irregular work flow, greater variability in work content, absence of data regarding the volume of work done in a day, absence of strict job specialization (both psychological and physical) provide a cumulative form of performance towards the side of employees. All these factors show disinterestedness and discontentment to them in the case of their job satisfaction. But their job satisfaction lies in various cases such as in case of taking care or marketing of sectors, marine products, ship-hyphen-repairing works, selling of paints to industrial users and selling of scientific equipments and wood products etc.

When all these factors are towards the employees performance, the leverage for individual need satisfaction in comparison to organizational need satisfaction has drastically increased therefore individual benefits are sought on all organizational decisions based on the following:

- Matching of individual and organizational needs has become more difficult.
- Rapid erosion in value and ethics.
- Demand for result orientation rather than activity orientation.
- Losing of talent due to luring by competitors.

- Increased job insecurity.
- Demand for getting the best pay packages.

Thus, the above mentioned ingredients highlights some crucial aspects. These aspects are being understood in consideration of the future scenario of all organizational components and its environment separately. Because, the management like a tight-rope walks and looks towards the importance of fulfilling employees needs when organizational goals are realized there. To elicit effective performance from the employees. It is necessary to listen their grievances and provide a satisfactory climate. But it follows in case of large organization, whereas in the case of small organization the management hardly need any elaboration.

There can be argued that the emerging picture regarding the supervisory behaviour of the management and treatment (meted out to employees) is, thus full of paradoxes. To some, they are found helpful and appreciative and to other, they are untrustworthy, irritating dictatorial and demanding.

In their connection, the organizations enable to maintain the following issues in creation of good relationship between the management and employees.

- Ensuring growth/development in future.
- Enabling the organization to cope with changes.
- Enabling the organization to become a learning organization.
- Optimum utilization of human resources.
- Low personnel expenses.
- Enabling (helping) the organization to become cost effective.
- Good, morale, motivation, and discipline.
- Belief in the organizational values, and strengthening the organizational values.

However, in view of examining mentioned facts, the management of the organization desires to ensure and stress on the availability of right manpower at right numbers, prompt grievance settlement, disciplined work force, flexibility in placement, adequate career development, rewards, increased power and involvement in human resource activities.

To overcome these problems, the organization give stress on the following : salary benefits to be the best, meaningful work, grievance settlements, not much restricting autonomy, no lay off, no wage cut, future growth, more security, more facility and also active participation in decision making.

Empowerment dwells upon delegated in the sphere of personnel's. The empowerment of employees are used widely in diversed context as power sharing with management for establishing a harmonious relationship between the employer and employees, to make understand the vistas of technology innovation accessing of information in relation to climate of industrial relation and realization of responsibilities for productivity to make improved flow of consumption.

Thus, the empowerment of employee's aims at involvement of workers in decision making with the management and to operate the elements in consequence of economic and social responsibilities. Such involvement implies realization of rational thoughts that make credibility and individuality—important factors for maintaining ideal industrial democracy with greater resulting in goodwill, mutual confidence and cooperatio's between the employees and the management. But this is possible to evince a socialistic pattern of society in case of performance, development and expansion of the enterprise. Because the empowerment of employees is considered for threshold of industrial and economic development to any developing country like India.

Thus, the empowerment of the employees advocates the participation of the working process of production with a view to give its due share. The share is used for sufficiency and efficiency in diversed form for achieving economic development. But the empowerment of employees must not be individualistic rather at should be collective.

The managers of any organization unit are found reluctant. Because they feel that employees are demanding a share of their authority and responsibility. They share in exercising their responsibilities by keeping responsibility and superiority before the employees of the enterprises.

Sometimes, the employees åre found in unwilling action though right decisions are made there. On such occasion they form delegation and share in managerial power. Their such delegation linked with social delegation heightens clout and power with their formation of group. Such situation creates congenial human relations between workers and managers.

Test Questions

1. What is employee's empowerment?
2. What are the necessary conditions for the empowerment of any organization?

14
Manpower Management in 21st Century

In fact, the part of the 21th century witnesses a gradual shift from the industrial economy to the information economy, where the information technology has revolutionised the ways of business with high level of transparency in imperative forms. There is not doubt that the Indian society is a highly diverse society consisted with wide spread poverty as well as existence of big middle class. In addition to, the society is related with more diverse and complex system economically, politically, sociologically and culturally. Such complexity shows an attribute of diverse people who have different needs, structure of education, role of technology, the present technological innovation in continuity and substantiality in performance. All these are changed systems where changes undergo in order to cope with the technological innovation, competitive understandings and optimistic functions. The functions are mainly concerned with the creation of various cross functional teams to examine the problems in holistic way and to coordinate the efforts of concerned functions, categorized changes of the 21st century.

The following factors may be assumed more influential and they have direct bearing on the functioning of Indian organisation in the years to come.

Economic Changes

Trade liberalization and globalization of economics have transformed global economic environment with challenge into the 21st century in generation of revenues and preparation of high intensive management as global or transitional organisations marked by innovative strategires, new products and service.

Technological Changes

The rapid pace of technological changes has given rise to improvements in products and services emerging continuous innovation and upgradation in order to cope with the changing business environment and for achieving excellence.

Changes in Information Technology

The greater evolution in the field of communication, networking and information technology that make the "geographical distance irrelevant and of limited consequence in business", by using powerful tools of the 21st century in creation of new opportunities and challenges. These challenges are to be managed by the manpower management in consequence of network, connectivity as well as information technology.

The Knowledge Economy

The key differentiators that would provide a competitive edge of the 21st century though it does not have physical assets but knowledge assiets and information. The 21st century corporate should use knowledge to remain competitive. The competition is considered for knowledge about customer preference throughout the world. The decision making asserts on parameter and critical attributes for determining considerable assignments. Thus, the 21st century can be hypothesized as knowledge enterprise that ought to be visualized by the management.

Changing Profile of Domestic Consumers

The manpower management of the 21st century found increased penetration of international media, rising purchasing power and availability of wider variety of products and brands evolved in consumer expectations and perceptions. The created brands given assurance to the manufacturers to win the customers franchise by offering the right mix of price, product differentiation, experience and service. Such assurance provides an attraction to fulfill served conditions in consequence of markets whether national or international. In this context, the manpower managements to look more positive and more productive approach to the emerging challenges with greater deal of hard work. The work gives the concept of right changes to have effective measures internally and externally to lead respective opportunities of changes. The respective opportunities bring people of diverse backgrounds and interests together in ways that provide fair and equitable opportunities to contribute their best, achieve personal goals and realize their full potential as suggested by Chauhan (1999).

Need for Appropriate Changes to the Indian Economy

To survive and thrive in the new environment to the Indian society, there are required appropriate changes in the four context areas of quality, costs, marketing and technology. These changes to the society would be more successful unless tthe human spirits are not energized and mobilized to follow new opportunities, creation and promotion of commitment as central aspects of changes are considered as pivotal force whose vitality and viability show witnesses to meet the challenges of the new millennium economy in consequence of global and local competitions.

Process of Change before the Manpower Management

Managing change is probably the single most important issue of all those who have undertaken the task of managing organisation. Undoubtedly, changes in the environment be it technological, economic, social or psychological, have placed greater demands on organization to be flexible, responsive and efficient as remarked by Nilkant & Ram Narayan (1998).

The process of changes are interrelated with various ingredients such as important preparatory step of planning, ability of individual, recognized forces of change and established results for suitable climate. The ability of change depends upon two important factors, viz; (a) the willingness to top executives to devote substantial time to the process; and (b) the recognition by top management of the normal human reaction to resist change and the need to adopt a strategy designed to overcome resistance.

In view of examining stated facts, there is required to establish suitable climate following top management towards excellence. But for establishing suitable climate the following: management staffing; compensation and benefits; communication; talent management and employee relations may be emphasised to set up the machinery for planning and implementing change in a way which encourage the maximum use of human resources. The resources are involved with changes to articulate the need for change, major transformational effort and high motivation and enthusiasm in continuation for exciting maximum benefits. But the benefits are an integral part of the management to the organization for generating commitment to change. Change strategies that follow a well defined sequence of steps are likely to be more successful that there are haphazardly implemented.

Thus in this regard, the manpower management should abide to tackle the problem of change process in providing effective capability to deal with change. It can also give the people a feelings of participation, achievement and self respect for change and articulate the roles of change sponser, agent and target.

However, a remark may be given that in addition to knowledge, intelligence and technical competence, leaders of future are required to adopt a holistic approach in managing change in their organization.

Management and its Functions in 21st Century

Management is creative problem solving. It works within the paradigm or within the system. It uses great number of instruments, methods and attitude in order to cope a competitive edge over competitors. It is easier to learn leadership with directive that requires to inspire people to give their best for achieving shared goals. It cannot be effective without the following combined qualities being present: natural drive, a thrust for adventure, courage, sense of reality, ambition, imagination, restive temperament, a fundamental respect as well as genuine interest (De wool 1994). Its leadership means (i) inventing new markets, (ii) changing the rules of the game in existing markets and (iii) changing the structure of industry through merger, acquisitions or joint ventures in order to create value for all the stake holders. Its function is to optimize the resources allocated where the optimization would be served in determination of different organizational subsystems synthesized with a common purpose for networking and facilitating human resource processes.

The processes are related to gender and cultural diversities for having sensitivity to the cultural norms of the community in achieving best results by means of formulated policies and sensitized the employees to the cultural demands. The demands require attraction and retention strategies that are to be designed accordingly with performed measurements and rewards around parameters which reflect the effective utilization of net over technology.

Examining all considerable factors as mentioned above, the annual report to inventor of 21st century will include qualification of 'intellectual capital' held by the organization and other measures like retention rates, due compliance levels, employee satisfaction indices.

Concludingly, the manpower management deals with quite exciting and challenging diversed resources for devising a new philosophy, new interventions, systems and policies, and relationship inside the organization and with suppliers and customers for changed environment in great deal of transformational measures and methods in the 21st century.

Need of Systematic Attention towards the Management

To any manpower management there has been visualised that foodgates should be open; profitable possibilities abound to achieve corporate goals, business leaders need their employees full attention and that attention is in short supply. The attention of the employees has been analyzed through three lenses—economic, psychological and technological. These components are the guidelines of keeping employees focused on crucial corporate tasks.

For solving the crucial problems to the management the organizations must have necessity for formalized systems of information's flow in cases of managerial functions of planning, operating and controlling. Because manager depend on the specific tool—the information and although they get things done through others, either through words or written statements. The need for information systems appear obvious to managerial decision-making. The decision is served as effective and competitive included with thought of integrated programme in consequence of following management principles, individual manager's style and behaviour and organization structure.

For fulfilling these conditions information technology has been found as the combination of four disciplines, viz., information science, computer technology, communication technology and management. Such combination serves in finding relationship between the computer and its use for managerial decisions emphasising on how the computer system makes programmed decisions and how it provides decision assisting information for complex decisions that do not lend themselves to automation.

Thus, manpower management critically based on evaluation, planning or decision-making is fraught with searches for information to handle the various crises that arise in addition to the normal work-flow. In this context, components have been used such as people, tasks, technology, culture and structure to the organisation.

The above concepts for developments components have been taken as measures for emphasizing improvement for organization's performance. These components stress the manager to take into account their interdependent relationship, particularly in case of major managerial challenge of information technology for developed information systems. The developed informations relate with various functions like operations/manufacturing, quality control, marketing and service. Operations/manufacturing include production scheduling, material planning, inventory control etc. which also follow an inclusion for product planning and control. The quality activities are product test and product control supported by materials handling, quality control and numerical control. Marketing and servicing consist of sales planning, sales analysis and advertising and the supporting activities that persue field operations and ware—housing. Also finance/administration functions consist of profit planning, capital budgeting, pay role, cost accounting, billing, personnel administration supported by attendance, reporting, labour reporting and dispatching.

Examining above mentioned facts, it is found that now the major systems are not separate and distinct, they connect, interact and otherwise tie the sub-systems of the organization together through the medium of information. It may also be noted in this specified case that these major systems serve to integrate the basic functions of planning, operating and controlling, must are designed and utilized primarily for one or two of these functions such that the results and discussions show the evidences in both non-programmed and programmed decisions.

Though decision is taken place with the whole lengthy and complex process of defining and exploring the many objectives in it. It does not consider literature and teaching, rather, it attempt to focus on the moment of decision. Because the system analysists and managers are to analyze the utilized information technology with the context of problem solving and systems design most extreme important factors.

Distinguishing extremity, the range of decision is assumed as programmed and non-programmed in order to cope with improvement of decision making processing two general approaches old and new to the techniques involved. These have been derived from the jargon of computer field, where a programme is defined as a plan for the automatic solution of a problem. Decisions lend themselves for programming techniques if they are repetitive and routine. A procedure can also be worked out for handling them so that each is neither an ad hoc decision nor one to be treated as new situation each time it arises.

Non-programmed and Programmed Decisions

Making distinction between two stated decision, non-programmed decision is unstructured, new, of high consequence elusive/complex or involves major commitments. This decision takes steps of advertised budget, new product decisions, acquisition and merger considerations, board member selection and similar problems are illustrated with devised rule to reach programmed approaches. The approaches are exercised by means of judgement which is used by a function of experiences, institution and insight. It is found that over the years, the executives are to urge to learn, practice and acquire the habit of making decisions based on the problem solving process, i.e., define, the problem-identification-choosing the best alternative. The identification concentrates on selection process devoted to past success but attempted to predict future success. Though the past achievement provides increased variation and also shows an evidence of creation of complexity that becomes difficult in making decision for future success in the case of any management.

The programmed decision reflects on various vital factors such as computed pay accorded to the agreement contact, organizational policies as well as regulations and also serves for pricing orders, credit checks and payment of accounts for daily purposes.

This decision is most prevalent technique in provision for indoctrinating the training of new personnel and for guiding experienced personnel in consideration of their performance with oriented approaches, scientific methods, real models based on quantitative measurements and techniques for making concentration on relationship between specified descriptions and business applications.

But this decision stands for solving many problems as possible on routine basis by using applicable models. The routine basis serves for greater relief to the management portrayed as a major force for organizational and managerial change.

Thus, information technology helps in computing powers and information advances which are likely to influence on managerial decisions to handle quantitative measures and operational level of business. The programmed decision performs its service towards marketing information by means of managerial functions based on three important factors viz, planning, operating and controlling to the manpower management in 21st century. Though there exist complex problems with high increased extensity but they are being accomplished through information technology in consequence of techniques of management science for automated decision assisting information.

Developed Principles Laid on Knowledge Management in 21st Century

The 21st century entails the knowledge management emerging as an important area of management thought and practice. The management recognized the knowledge as the quintessential resource for continuous competitiveness in systematic and integrative process of coordinating organization. The coordination is undertaken with widened activities of acquiring, creating, storing, sharing, diffusing, developing and deploying all sorts of knowledge by means of transformation and integration of raw information's. These factors show their significance in creation of an interactive learning environment for solving problem, innovation and novelty, identification for new knowledge and determination of the knowledge management.

The knowledge in systematised from to any organisational management adheres to purpose, direction, business model and the logic of its customer value proposition. The proposition is formulated and implemented principles indicating dynamism and flexibility for outcome of holistic, fluid, unstructured, iterative and creative process of thinking. Strategic thinking involves consideration of various possibilities, different alternatives, desired/envisioned goals, probable and plausible outcomes. The outcomes are related with structured decision varying time horizons, indefinite planning, scheduling of actions available in light of vision and values. They are taken into consideration of focal perspectives and enable to interpret certainty and reality corresponded to business affairs in varied magnitudes.

The vision defines the purpose and direction of an organization when purpose approaches towards structure system in order to cope audacious goals and stimulated organism to actualise the organisation's vision or strategic intent to the organizational unit. The management must adhere to coherent and reasoned perspective on an evolution of the industry within which the form is located to any area.

For the 21st century, the located firm must be evolved with unique value propositions specifying operational excellence, product leadership, and customer intimacy indicating threshold level of market acceptable performance at the most convenient and competitive price for building up position and values in innovation in form of cyclic order. The value is mainly associated with identification of expertise, skills, competencies and capabilities for reaching best approaches of structures around providing best in class customer value, and enhancing the same year after year.

In addition to, the said century entails the designed business following position and profit that are outcomes to salient dimensions of a firm management in respect of business design. The dimensions are basically interrelated with consideration of value profitably, value capture, differentiation/strategic control and scope for determination of nature, context and direction of the firm's business strategy forming defined strategy, specified customer segments and profits models in required and balanced scorecard.

Giving concentration on balanced scorecard. If it found as a holistic set of inter-linked measures that derive performance. It also centers on and grows out of a company's vision for achieving success in delivering superior value to the customer in view of customer perspective, internal operations perspective, innovation as well financial perspective. The perspective is used in inclusion of measures pertaining to time, quality, service, cost and customer perception and base. The perspective also gives the concept relating to improvement, intellectual assets and learning as a whole in an indication of shares to the employees, whereas financial perspectiveness gives the measures of profitability, growth and shareholder value.

Thus, the balanced scorecard emphasises focuses on establishing a balance between financial and non-financial measures for creating and achieving an overall congruence of goals. Such directives show the significance for the results based on strategy of management in framing and clarifying the nature and dimension of the enterprise.

Basic Types of Management Strategy

In fact, the literature of management in voluminous forms attributes formulated strategy that approaches in rich forms, particularly stressing of the management emphasizes on efficiency in producing products at low-cost and finding ways and means of supplying the produced items to the customers in easier form without showing created hardship. So in tackling this problem, the management made its efforts to differentiate strategy in consideration of customer segments or market riches. For differentiated strategy there exists an innovated strategy in varied degrees that also involves new products/services in creation of redesigning its business processes emerging a creation of effectiveness and competitiveness in the market towards the side of producer of the product.

Considerable Characterised Feature Relating to the Manpower Management in 21st Century

The three considerable features performance, adaptation and opportunity that specify characterisations of management in 21st century.

The first component performance refers to a firm's inferior performance as compared to the performance of its more successful competitors. The second component adaptability refers to the firm's relative inability to change its structure, functions and processes and its inadequate capability to acquire and use new knowledge, skills competencies, and technology in the light of changing business conditions. The third component 'opportunity' refers to the firm's failure to envisage and exploit new business opportunities for creating a new trajectory of growth. These three components have to be addressed continually and concurrently in creation of effective management of the firm. They also overcome the situation arising due to reasons of employee's empowerment, cross-functional teams, drive down decision making to lower levels and devise appropriate incentive and reward systems for improving performance.

Besides above three components, there are required sustained and relentless cultivation of learning and continual development, sharing and use of knowledge for problem-solving and value generation, cost efficient operations and creation of new competitive space which relate an minextricable linkage between managing strategy and knowledge of the firm. But the question arises that what type of knowledge of the firm exists there. The knowledge considers the strategy consisting of categorized terms in an indication of right form of directive principles applicable to firms size, location and scale in accordance with the context of operations and models of business.

The mentioned factors in collaborative linkages and alienated forms provide firm's current and planned initiatives/projects in terms of their objectives, rationales, progress and priorities of high significance to pursue the strategy naturally and logically. The pursued strategy of the management must be needed to recognize, specify and organize in light of finding close examination, evaluation and changes, of all aspects of business environment. But capitalizing on environmental change is the essence of entrepreneurship. Knowledge of environmental change is vital for recognition of opportunities.

Thus, a management in accuracy and adequacy reveals to draw up a strategy for augmenting the potential of human resources in making identification of areas and human resources for developed economy of any country to cater to the growing demands for industry in the new millennium.

Management in Today's Economy with Reference to India

The present day management provides a brand marketing as scientific perhaps to compete with the term scientific management. The scientific management specifies a frame of mind, which reuses to accept past practices. It means substituting a rule of thumb by a more thought-out plan action. This management is also defined as collection of data to support decision.

Referring the Indian economy, the context being "management in today's economy", is clearly in the doldrums. There is no indication that the planned objectives for removal of poverty and the simulation of growth with price stability will be achieved. The progress has been uneven. No doubt, a good foundation is being laid for important industries like steel, heavy engineering and fertilizers though not exactly at a pace. But the growth of agriculture and of the consumer industry has been patchy. The per capita availability of the basic necessities of life have not kept pace with demand. The result is that prices are ruling high. This is also the case with raw materials and power.

Also, the economic scene is overshadowed by inflation, a world wide phenomenon owing to the like in some specific commodities prices. The spurt in inflation is a cumulative result of past performances and action. The process has gone up even at a faster rate. But it is equally imperative production and productivity should be improved by utilizing our capacity and resources better.

Examining the economy of the country, it is believed that marketing. concept has gained universal acceptance, not at least, as a philosophy of business. There are many businesses, both large and small, who believe that marketing has no place on economy of shortages. To them production is all important. That means to say that production receives all their attention and marketing none. It has been argued in many instances that in a controlled economy marketing has little validity. Implicitly, the company's existence follows in finding its ability to satisfy at least some aspects of the consumer demand. The consumer needs are being assessed by the marketing, which is itself a creative management function. The function indicates the economic objectives that one viewed in terms of return on investment, price earning ratio, volume of business, size of operations, liquidity, reduction in the share of the market and so on giving stress on more maximization of profits rather that customer satisfaction.

The corporate sectors are witnessing tremendous changes thanks to the liberalisation of the Indian economy. The pressure is mounting on the Indian industry to perform-produce quality goods and afford causality services. The competition is escalating and there is the crying need to become cost effective, upgrade work methods, work norms, technical and managerial skills and employee motivation to task up the gauntlets. Consequent upon this one can expect manifold cultural and economic changes of great import in human resource management in the coming years.

Test Questions

1. What are the responsible factors to bring changes in the functioning of Indian organisation?
2. Assess the future of HRM in India.

15

The Emerging Profile of Human Resources

Human Resources Strategy

This study reveals a high degree of change in process in which organisations achieve the linkage between HRM function and the strategic management. The strategic management is considered to meet the challenges from international competitors, though economic conditions, macro economic reform and restructure of management practices are emphasised on linkage of human resources strategies with organisational strategies—an organisational strategies consistent with resource-based view of an enterprise.

In this connection, Dyer (1984) suggested that human resources management is identified by the domain of the research, differentiating between the content or process of HRM strategy. The strategic HRM is, thus, defined as the process in which human resources strategies have been used to enable an organisation to achieve its strategic objectives.

The strategic objectives are considered in the following: emphasis on the strategic integration of people issues with corporate strategies: consistent with the resource based view of the enterprise, integration is being achieved by external fit (i.e., fitting structure, systems, and management practices to the organisation's stage of development) and internal fit (i.e., the HRM department's structure, systems and management practices in terms of complement.)

In identification of strategic plan of HRM there is carried in sight in human nature between industrial relations and personnel administration.

In defining levels of factors, 'administrative' linkage is similar to the traditional personnel management model where there does not exist any relationship between HRM and the strategic management process. 'One-way' linkage is characterized by either the HRM function or strategic planning function, imposing an overall influence on the direction of HR strategies. The next level 'two way' linkage has a strategic characteristic, as there is two-way process between HR and business strategies. Finally, the 'integrative' linkage is similar to that of an ideal strategic HRM state where the HRM has a key role in strategic management process.

In light of historical perspective of integration, Golden and Ramanujam (1985) have illustrated that integration factors can be grouped into two broad categories, viz., organizational specific and HR function specific factors. These integration factors have been derived from research in the USA and a few researches have been conducted to determine the appropriateness of these factors in the Australian context.

Use of Strategic HRM

It is function of factors such as (i) size of the firm, (ii) overall sophistication in the use of business planning, (iii) involvement of HR managers in the business planning process; (iv) intensity of research and development activities and (vi) stability of organisation's employment.

Thus, human resources-important practices are used to transform from their existing role to one which is strategic and flexible. They should change their individual perspective towards HRM function and acquire a strategic mindset, recognising the HR can be used as a source of competitive advantage. To enable this shift, they must recognize the need to change. In order for HR practitioners to exhibit a shred mindset, they must be willing to undertake change and a self-realisation that change is essential in the process. The self-realisation is the process for providing stimulation to the new role.

New roles competencies in HRM must be acquired to add value to the organisations. Because HRM competencies are understood, such as (i) good business understanding; (ii) shared mindset between HRM and the rest by the organisation; (iii) strategic thinking capability; (iv) functional capability—excellence in the delivery of day-to-day HRM activities; (v) response to change and the ability to act accordingly; and (iv) movement towards customization of HR products and services.

So far as employment stability is concerned, it does not provide any implication to the strategy of human resources management due to reasons of unionization, specialization and corporatisation of the organization in the early 1990's. The term 'corporatisation' has been introduced as a volatile commercial market environment emphasizing on structures and employment levels which are found in perceived results. However, strategic HRM is actively adopted as a means of meeting the challenges placed on the traditional public service culture which has been enshrined within the organization. On the other hand, a high turnover and the competitive nature of the commercial banking and IT sectors did not provide motivation to adopt strategic HRM within the respective organizations. Because there are some important factors such as firm size, strategic planning, and formality of HRM systems and processes which are more influential in determination of organisation's adoption of strategic HRM. The HRM practitioners have to be effective in balancing their different roles. They are required to be strategic business partners to line managers, deliver HR products and services, and provide consultancy to line managers.

Thus, giving light on HRM policies; there must be determined the extent of consistencies during internal (horizontal) integration by an adoption of effective review of the strategic HRM process in order to make identification of new techniques and approaches from the realm of social science to develop and hypotheses are to be tested there with formulation and implementation.

Role of Human Resources in the Business Environment of Next Millennium

The role of human resources in a new paradigm of business is to be redefined as the next millennium following challenging tasks caused by various changes such as global competition, downsizing and technological advances. These factors exist due to changes of work place and socio-cultural values accounting for across the globe where human resources are used for organizational growth and development in determination of problems and issues related to the work force, human capital managing, knowledge, assets management, and development of intellectual capital. These factors are very essential for progress and developments of organisation emphasising on plan, envision, priorities and setting goals for themselves.

However, human resources are used to understand the challenges and realities of the business, so that they can facilitate a smooth transition of organization and workforce in the next millennium. In this context, human resources personnels have to do a strategic analysis of the change taking place in the business environment to build organisation capacity to maximize the potential of the business in the market place. Though their role in the past held a pivotal but there will be their critical role in the next century as we move forward. Because their role is recognized from administrative to strategic business partner in respect of diverse workforce as well as changes in the environment.

Human Resources Evolution

The social and business history reveals that 'human resources professional' working under the banner of "professional" always worked to improve working conditions, business practices, job satisfaction, and workers productivity. They have made tremendous contribution of the free enterprises system—an important function in the organisation. Though the activities of human resources involved from the beginning of the 20th century to the date is being explained below for greater changes - nature of job of human resources professionals, and their role in organizational growth and development.

Era of Blue Collar Factory Workers (1920-1930)

This could be characterized as emergence of automobile, steel and cement industries usually for few established departments at the workplace and psychological testing and employee counselling started there. Following these conditions, company canteen, pension benefits, and life insurance practices were created in very enthusiastic forms.

Era of Great Depression (1930-1940)

In this era unionisation started picking up where personnels were heavily engaged in setting improved wages, working conditions, handling grievances, emphasising on devised techniques such as employees empowerment, and psychological factors in motivations through employee communication programmes as well anti-unionisation.

Era of World War II (1940-1950)

This era stressed personnel department into two, viz., (i) Industrial Relation which managed union contracts and (ii) Personnel to manage people and increase workforce productivity. During this phase various schemes such as employee pension, health plan and other benefit programmes have been considered as measurable steps through employee communication and unionisation.

Era of Post War Economy (1950-1960)

In post war period, more employment was generated in manufacturing sector with the emergence of white-collar worker. Due to emergence of white-collar worker the personnel functions were found more systemized in consequence of supervisory training (role play and sensitivity training), professional ethics and career development programme for both male and female workforce.

Era of Human Relation Movement (1960-1970)

It was a time of psychological orientation at work place—bonus, employees suggestion scheme, performance management programme, participatory management programme and merit based pay programme for workforce of both sexes.

Era of Challenging Task (1970-1980)

Having found challenging tasks relating to satisfaction to employees of the organisation they explore the following (a) competence; (b) mobility in labour market; (c) movement for civil right and (d) initiation of enriched programmes. Thus, the term personnel was converted into 'Human Resources'.

Era of Restructuring and Re-engineering (1980-1990)

After 1980, downsizing, quality circles, task forces, team building and employee involvement programmes were started due to various reasons such as economic downturns international competition, technology changes and outplacement and also restructuring of the organization. During this phase, human resources personnel's had to deal several problems at workplace, such as sexual harassment, work/family issues, workforce diversity and AIDS. Thus, this phase recognized 'human resources' as the only source of competitive advantage.

Era of Post-Modern Organisation (1990 and afterwards)

In the post-modern industry society employees need flexibility in all areas of work are being given due considerations. The considerations in human resources are characterised as planning, employees rights, flexible benefits and computerization of human resources related information. On the eve of the 21st century the enterprises are struggling with the issues of downsizing, productivity and global competition in making attribute of human personnels who are to have concentration. On cutting edge of human resources practices to survive and to be successful in the knowledge-based economy.

Thus, this phase changed human resources concept to have an exploration of the nature of work environment, issues related to workforce and workplace due to reengineering, restructuring and downsizing efforts in the business environment. The changes have been brought in terms of flexibility, managing a diverse workforce, women and minorities, entry into work force, sexual harassment. AIDS, and international work force which perform greater contribution to the organizations through better human resources management.

Though it is very ticklish to predict future. Still people endeavour to foretell future. At least, for visualising a possible normal trend in the series and events and a probable normal trend in the chain and events and a probable path to managers are keenly interested in implementation of personnel in human resource management. The management shows the ethical code totoe regulate the behaviour of the members of the profession. Thus, if managers are to boost productivity, reduce costs, and improve their organisation competitive trend, they must focus on how to properly manage people. The personnel management of human resource is an engrossing and fast changing subject. Human resource management has undergone stupendous changes in the past generations. The next generation will usher changes from the days when manager houred the subordinates with a stop watch and threats of punishment. The ambience in which managers work today is more dynamic than in past. And the individuals with thrilling challenges and opportunities for managing an organisation's most prized resource, its people.

The following concerned rates are worth noting to predict changes that will occur within the next decade.

(1) ***Gravest concern for human resource management*** **:** During 1970's human resource management had a peripheral role. Today human resource management has a momentous role to play. And human resource managers have acquired more power thanks to escalating labour cost, concern for improving worker productivity, quest for compensation plans which motivate and the crying need for interpreting and implementing government rules.

The future human resource managers will learn how to employ their novel power. They will turn powerful decision makers and will have responsibilities that will go with greater influence. Moreover, owing to growing significance of human resource management senior executives in the organisation will be increasingly springing from human resources management function. In future ambitious executives will employ human resource management as the springboard to the top instead of traditional functions like engineering, production, finance or marketing.

(2) ***The waiving of 'termination' as threat*** **:** Legislation has heaped lots of burden on the employer to make a justification of termination of an employee on some legitimate scores. This trend along with greater demands by unions gave guarantee to life time employment. The oriented employment with higher skill recognises potential development in decision making to factor goal human relations.

(3) ***The bi- modal force :*** Growth in the work force will be confined to two extremes of the income spectrum. There will be a massive demand for the educated professionals who earn hefty salaries and among low-skilled workers who eke out the minimum wages. The future work-force will incline towards bimodal distribution:

(i) Two large groups with different wage rates.

(ii) Two large groups relating to men-workers and women-workers.

The implications of this trend will be that major salary and benefit changes will have to be made to reflect and adjust this bimodal workforce. Competition among companies for the skilled workers will shoot up. The policy of upgradation to employees interacts in dynamism of organisation for performing high skillness. Then, more co-operative arrangement between business and universities can be expected. Owing to bimodal nature of work-force tension between high wage earners and low wage earners will brew. To motivate a low wage service worker will be a major challenge especially through employee participation and non-financial rewards. Various kinds of tensions will mount up amongst the men and women group of workers, especially in relation to distribution of responsibilities and moral behaviours.

(4) *Dual Career Couples* : The dual culture among employees (men and women) would be inclined towards low mobility and decreased inflated trends in organisational structure. The greater number of dual career couples will decrease the mobility of the employees. There will be greater resistance to promotional offers that need geographical moves. Organisations will also have to implement better human resource planning systems.

(5) *Move to make organisation uniform* : There is an increasing trend among organisations to remove middle levels from their big structures and make them flat in order to pare cost and render faster decisions.

The implications of this trend will be: Organisations will start dehiring employees. Career growth opportunities will have to be provided. The emphasis will be put on out placement services in the organisation.

The sense of commitment and loyalty to organisation will suffer tremendously. Employees will become more self-oriented.

(6) *Computer at home* : By using personal computers at home workers will process information and more people will have employment opportunities more work will be disposed of at home by employees. And persons who need flexibility in time schedule owing to their kids and older persons who wish to increase their income after retiring from services will be doing work at home that was once done on the premises of the companies. Hence, home working will be causing a major restructuring in pay levels. The companies will have to determine the potential of each job and pay accordingly. The reaching potentiality devices resultants in determination of quality control steps. Close supervising of work will not be a possibility hence performance evaluation will have to be revised. Monitoring techniques will be developed for ensuring accuracy and punctuality in work culture.

(7) *Benefits and health* : A new trend has developed to attract good female employees. The general trend it has that woman workers work harder and do not create any political problems in the organisation. Hence, the organisations will furnish expanded day-care benefits in future.

The implication of this trend will be: The payment for day-care services will hike organization's costs. And to be in the competitive stream organisations will be forced to offer this as a benefit. Non-smoking will be implemented at work place. Companies will afford gym facilities and health clubs to the members. Time offs from workload will improve health of employees.

(8) *Decline of unions* : The number of workers who join unions exhibits a decreasing trend in various countries including India. Thanks to bi-modal distribution of work force, there will be fewer employees joining unions. Women workers refrain from involving in union activities. However, unions will shift focus on low-skilled workers.

The implications of this trend will be : Despite union's action, the animosity between the management and union will increase on the score of discrimination between educated professionals and minimum wage services workers.

(9) *Matching the milieu to the employee ergonomics* : There is a growing trend among organisations to make a study of work environment, space-utilization, office furniture and provision of different facilities to provide a productive area specially to lessen stress and strain and create a congenial and salutary work station.

Organization's efforts for new decorations, office furnishings, space-utilization and facility provisions will make employee's ambience more laborious and healthy and this environment will be conducive to their working. The work related healthy problems will be reduced to great extent by managers.

(10) *Employee rights* : It will have the same trend in future too. The employer's right to lay off workers has been regimented by law: The employee terminations have been constrained by law. The upshot of these limitations will increase in oneness and complexity for human resource manager.

However, in conclusion of given study there revealed that the post liberalized era can be characterized as generating more employment opportunities and higher standards of living. There is found greater change in worker's profile by finding indications of age, gender, religion, caste, language, culture, ethnicity, and education—all these factors are witnessing for demographic studies of the workers and related to creative and flexible work environment. The flexible work environment includes telecommuting, flexible time schedules, virtual office, alternative work week, work at home, compressed work-week, voluntary reduced hours, and cultural work contributing self-creation and self-sustaining for maintaining peace, mental health, and career momentum of workers in a global village.

For such greater changes, organizations prefer a flatter structure. Managers are acting as facilitators. Workers are going to be partners in industry. They will be driven by intrinsic values. Loyality has been replaced by competence and employees are being empowered to take decisions and have greater degree of autonomy. In addition to microelectronics and latest communication tools such as e-mail, fax, pagers and internet technologies have totally revolutionized the world of work with the result the difference in time and space has also shrunk.

In this context, human resources professionals have to look for opportunities to acquire within the organization and to make top management understand the importance of 'human resource'. They have to achieve organizational goals through development of human resources give stress on functional knowledge and diagnostic skill, strong self concept, personnel influence, tactical planning and result orientation for creating multi-skilled workforce to organizations aligned with human resources strategies through training, education and development programmes.

Test Questions

1. Describe the future of human resources management in India.
2. Test the future role of HR managers.
3. Briefly discuss the implications of changes in the vistas of technology, environment and people.

16

Special Features of New Technology

In consideration of new technology, the process and consequence of introducing new technology vary from one organization to another. A technology system is more than the sum of its techniques depending upon consecutive success as earmarked by several cultures in respect of technological changes. The substantive change establishes organization structure, job design and required skills, values, attitudes for one or more than one factor followed by behaviour of employees. Though these factors have been studied by several authors concerning with technological changes. In this context (Dawson, 1994) and (Aldag et at 1994) have mentioned that substantive change in one or more or the above factors. Leads to perceived or actual psychological threat of job displacement, reduction in economic security, disruption of social transformations for arrangements and redefining of authority relationship. These threaten the psychological and social status of an employee triggering off resistence to change.

The experience of bringing new technology has been mixed in emerging economies like India. Technologies like computer controlled machines (CCM) and Advanced Manufacturing Technology (AMT) increased to the cost of administration in certain organization rather than streamlining the system or improving the productivity

(Dutta1990).

In this connection, Dayal and Aggarwal 1995 have pointed out that the success of new technology is found in emerging the extent to which the workforce is ready to accept and adopt to the technological as well as to the organisational changes. Though western technologies have been perceived in general workers and users supports to the technological changes, but their reaction to subsequent organizational changes is mixed proposing a model or transition that highlights. 'People' as a critical organizational factor. Their model is being assumed in making identification of knowledge and skills of the employees with this study, Pasmore and his colleagues (1982) have stated based in 134 studies of technology that change reveals the productivity and the importance of non-technical feature of "enduser" in improvement of organizational productivity. For an elaborated study of technological perspective, several researchers focussed on attitude and motivation following interplayed variables to the organisation.

Because, in observation, there is found that employee attitude is a key variable that must be considered in order to explain and predict the degree of success of technological change in an organization. But there is need for effective instrument evolving the attitude of employees towards technological change to the organization.

Need for the Instrument

The need for this new instrument has been considered due to following reason; (a) focus, on the contents of many instruments, on-organizational variables (like organizational structure work tasks and skills) rather than end-user variables (like opinions, fears and apprehensions, and (b) lack of measurements that measure psychological reaction of attitude. In this regard, existing literature emphasizes the link between technological change and organizational systems, using the psychological outcome or response of the employee as implied rather than directly tested. Though most of the studies did make any indication concerning the role of the individual worker as a moderator between technological change inputs and their outcomes. However, the main focus has been on the inputs of technological change (independent variables) and outputs of change (dependent variable). There is a need to identify worker related to psychological variables that can affect the outcomes of change.

During the change process, 'trying out or experiencing' stage the evaluation takes, place and opinions and attitude get formed. If the experience is negative, it decreases the likelihood of actual adoption of technological system and attitude can get revised downward.

The most important activity of the organisation is to know the attitude of members of the profession in determination of needs to the organisation. The needs recognise in diversed forms. Thus, in order to understand worker's reaction to technological change besides the organisational context it is equally imperative to study their attitude towards technological changes. For technological change their has been assigned the instrument in the form of Likert-type attitudinal scale that has been developed for the purpose of assessing employees attitude towards the change at the personal level and job content level in terms of confirmatory analysis revealing high internal consistency. By making conformation in analysing facts, there appears to find validity and reliability in assumed differentiable variable.

Technological Change Concerning Indian Organisation

This study would give light on Indian Organisation representing all shades of organisational evolution to build high level of productivity. In view of examining mentioned ingredients following propositions may be undertaken into consideration for framework for making effectiveness of the organisation. Because it is only the integration of employees 'technical excellence and social needs and values which can create social capital for sustainable productivity.'

Propositions

1. The driving force is to develop spread ideas concerning human values for technological progress to regulate behaviour of members of the organisation.
2. Such efforts are counted in springing up spontaneously when the employees of the organization take steps in realization of organisation needs, interest and values.
3. Employees need may follow in varied forms such as safe, hygienic and satisfactory service and working conditions

following transcending personal growth and meaningful life. For achieving meaningful life, the organisation stresses on routine and reliable high quality innovative performance by the employees team work and creation of social capital emphasizing on increased competitive features and improved organisational productivity.

4. The cultural organisation provides incentives to extended form of mutual considerations to faster positive responses in the organisation.

5. The positive response creates a centric organisation in order to induce benevolent paternalism, familism, nurturance and personalizing relationships to let the employees feel that they are part of a longer family, where the employer and the employee cure for each other.

6. The organisation immenses technological progress to the members of the profession to communicate essence of technological excellence. The essence favours integrity and character with justice and fair play.

7. The employees of the organisation are socially and culturally bound to have strategic considerations made by the organisation in respect of various factors such as strong professionalism, self-driven team work, technological excellence and strategic thinking constituting Indian collectivist culture, trusting and personalized relationship.

8. The relationship between the organisation and its employees shows relative power and influence over the employees by means of appropriate systems and procedures involved in constituting integrated formations.

9. The integrated formation is taken an interplay of leadership between the organisation and its employees for making a caring organisation culture where organisational goals and objectives, systems and procedures, employees need and expectations are evolving symbolic pattern of management.

Thus, the technological excellence perceives a caring organization in the Indian systems not only for the well being of its employees, but also reaches an outstanding results to the people surrounding the organization and extending a helping hand to them is giving contribution to the society at large. That means to say, the technological excellence shows an attribute of different components following: capability of strategic problem solving, high technical competence, intimation of understanding of framed policy, and continued upgradation of knowledge for latest innovations. All these are related to the receptivity to local conditions, legal, socio-economic and political milieu, and above all the cultural values and employees needs and expectations. These factors are involved in coordination, control, strengthening of cultural imperatives and uniqueness of local conditions yielding high professionalism, competitiveness, efficiency and contractual relationship with employees.

Further, a concentration is made on the application of technological changes in case of organisation. The following are the cases where technological excellence provides its contribution:

(a) In examining the difference between large and small organizations in terms of structure, communication and effectiveness.

(b) In observing the cumulative and independent effect in terms of structure, communication and effectiveness in small and large organizations.

(c) In observing the cumulative and independent effect on individual and organisational level effectiveness between small and larger organisations in terms of structure and communication.

New Technology and Aid Novelty

The new technology shows an attribute of cost and efficiency afforded to existing worker of any organization. It shows a movement for economical allocation of the work. It stresses on technologies as automated processing such as computer controlled machines information processed by electronic equipments.

The technologies have been improved for plant utilization to advanced manufacturing systems of the developed countries.

Elasticity and Flexibility

The elasticity during production process must be maintained. Such maintenance is accounted during custom building products. Flexibility is also used for provision of changing of terms, terminologies and coded words during the production process. They must be switched in making the specification information in coded system.

Information in Coded System

The new technology stresses on coded information that make division for the distribution of the items whether in store, production process or delivery process, subject to the condition of minimum cost.

Responses of Time

The most effective measures for upgraded work whether in managerial skills or employees motivations must be kept for the following. Modification for old skills, flexible operation for rapid changes, receipt of immediate control data, operation of information technology systems and controlled measures for establishment & measurement.

The considerable factors of human resources are determined by well planned information technologies for organization that are to be effective and competitive in today's dynamic business environment indicating proper integrations among various systems. They interact between one factor to another.

Thus, the main effects and interactions for the environment (Management and chart programme) of any organization show the requirement of prime reasons to both superior and subordinates of the institutions. With the application of new technology the plants are found affected in handy situations for the absorptions of possible ingredients.

Test Questions

1. What are the features of new technology?
2. What are the reasons for introducing new technology?
3. What impact has fallen by new technology on people?

17

Concept and Process of Technological Innovations

Dubin stated concept of technological innovation in two important forms (a) formulated tools, instruments and awareness of technologies, and (b) fundamental and rational approaches with relative objectives. The explanation of the technological devices has been performed in single and uniform forms. Such information has adhered for evolutionary process. The evolution creates attainment of new devices. In this connection, Luther remarked about specific technologies concerned with handicraft, mechnisation and most production with devices of automation. Because the automation relates to industrial revolution and weeds out the human operator from the industrial scene. In this regard, human being is needed to play a pivotal role in the present automated technologies.

The modern technology zeros in change and integration. Technological developments are occurring so rapidly that they engender social problems. The absorption of technology implies novel types of organization, novel styles of supervision, new reward systems and a plethora of allied changes.

Modern Technology spawns a process of interdependence. It shapes human relations and generates co-operation and a community of interest on the part of a work group.

Technology revolutionises the occupation. The ratio of white collar workers to blue-collar workers has escalated the skill and intellectual requirements of the entire work force. The requirements of skilled personnel necessitate the accent on education in order to increase the highly developed manpower.

The new technology has wielded a greater impact on labour. Some has induced competency for development within the roles synergizing the competencies as well as mentoring the competencies for creating external and internal environmental process.

The new technologies of the present time furnish retaining of displaced individuals for any organized work in subordination of recognised factors. The factors allows individuals to work in missionary forms that are essentially needed to the developed organisation.

Process of Technology Innovations

The term 'technological innovations' are being used in modern work systems. Such system exists rapidly in consequences of selected problems absorption of new technologies, encompassed processes of new types of organisations and greater aspirations to supervisors during the time of supervision.

Red Tapeism is a procedural side, which merits control because of its delaying and harassing tactics. Sometimes there may be fictitious Red Tape when people are not aware and they are subject to it. This can be contained by developed outlook amongst the persons concerned. Genuine Red Tapeism may result from unnecessary checks set up by managers who fear from dealing work. In such a crucial situation the panacea lies in good leadership. They may stem from process which were useful earlier but still persist despite outliving their utility. This is an example of resistance to change. This procedure has become a habit for the persons who hate changes. The other cause for useless procedure is the fact that it is governed by authority who fail to understand the problems being engrossed in the work and the workers betray hesitation to pose a challenge to it.

Thus, technologies transformed into developed technologies exist for changed problems in operation of Red Tepeism. They pose challenge to human dignity and undermine the weakness. The difficulties in complex forms to human beings are found in complication. The developed trend and significant changed values in technologies make an identification of major psychological and social difficulties in admixture of industrial civilisation for meaningful process of works.

These factors provide inter-relationship among used and valuable factor to the work systems.

The psychological problem that plagues frustration, which escalates with lower skills and with less educated workers. The worker develops obsessing thinking because the work has been so simplified that it does not imply his full heed and tends to be involved in his personal problems.

In order to overcome the human effects of poorly designed systems the system experts and industrial engineers may be given training in human relations. The attempts are being made to fashion job systems which are suitable for people.

The process of new technology has been induced to made strength of cultural imperative, which is often inversely related to the (scope) extent of integration of national and international economies. This process of new technology contributes significant result based on greater integration of national and international economies related to cultural influences and also capital flow more freely across the national boundaries. These factors would constitute results for creation of convergence of national and international perspectives. The perspectives focus on the future for visualization of successful organization to the next millennium. The conception of any organisation is mainly related with consumers growing demands to attain competitive edge. The competitive edge can be clarified in manifestation of the quality, price scheduled delivery that permeates philosophy of relationship for marketing process sustained profitability and credibility.

The concept of new technology has been brought in the sense for having relative protected and isolated economy as well the market. It plans controls, coordinates and promotes industrial activities emphasizing the organisation in order to cope competitive and effective management accorded to the market for assessing a development role.

The development role required ".....that technological, strategic and structural choices need to be made by the organization keeping in view not only the interests of the organization, but also the development needs of the nation". Though the developmental needs exist in different phases in different forms for different aspects such as ownership, size, location and leading organizations. The Indian organizations have adopted western technologies—underlying principles, systems of management, ranging from manpower planning, recruitment, training, appraisal, reward system, delegation, communication, grievance handling, and so on.

In other words, the organisations located in our country took a cultural detour to remain effective. The cultural detour reflected the collectivist social values, some of which are delineated to be a preference for (a) embededness in groups such as family case and other collectives, (b) arranging ideas, opinion, relationships, and all other conceiable, tangible and intangible things hierarchically, (c) maintaining a personalized relationship. Adopting a moralistic orientation to discharge duties and meet obligations to the family, friends, and relatives and maintaining harmony and tolerance among intergroup members by fostering cooperation among the employees. And blending them with nutrient management in determination of effectiveness of the organisation for realizing high productivity in terms of stimulated economic activities.

Dynamism in Process of Technological Innovations

"Process of Technological innovations" is considered as "change" moving from present state to a desired state in response to dynamic internal factors. Growth takes place only through the force of change. The force of change attributes technology, economic conditions, global competition, world politics, social and demographic changes as well as internal problems involved in the organisation.

As changes in organisation are stimulated by multiple external and internal forces, in order to survive and prosper, must respond and adapt to these forces. They must innovate continuously and improve their products and services to meet changing customer demands and competition for changed environment in determination of strategic formulations and their adoptions in process of technological changes to the organization.

Technologies must be updated and new and better ways to organise and manage for any organization. The individual managers and organizations that recognize the invitability of change and learn to adapt will be most successful as pointed by Cook and others in the year 1997. It is true that although the change is inevitable and perhaps there are some constant things in the world, that are always resistance to change.

Resistance can take place either at the individual level or at the organisational level. At the individual level resistance is caused due to selective perceptions, lack of communication, fear of the unknown and resentment towards the initiator, organization too resist change for most of the same reasons as individuals do.

Usually, it has been observed that during changes in decision making, authority and control of resource allocation, there is required the balance of power in organisations. Units benefiting from the change endorse it, but those losing power resist it. But organisations resist change when there is a structural stability due to change—since basically structures, rules and regulations are designed to develop consistent, and predictable behaviour. An organisation is a system of interrelated structure and subsystems. A change in any area .

However, for finding greater degree of changes in the organization, there are required education and communication that follow changes consecutively. Such consequence provide an acceptance of changes in very graceful manners in order to cope participation and involvement in changing process. Such processes minimises resistence extra considerations. Thus, the following factors: support, taining, consulting etc. may reduce resistence. Also regotiation and agreement are often important tools for dealing with powerful resistors.

For learning, the process of technological changes, have been brought at different levels to the members of the organisation such as:

- The first level acquiring values attitude, beliefs, principles, knowledge and skills.
- The second level mentions activity where elements are acquired there in finding actual performance to make comparison during

feeding back and intending performances.

- Reflection, the third level, involves questioning, and analyzing about how things work and overcoming assumption. It is free of external action. It may lead to redeeming the way one conducts business.
- The fourth level consists of learning for combined things and actions accorded to the principles of developed strategy, allocated resources and actions taken given emphasis on desired changed results indicating a high impact of application of learning.
- The fifth level shows the significance of small learning that is to be reinforced for creating efforts during the process of changes particularly in terms of integration personal and financial performance to solve present problems and to have a good prediction of future subject to conditions of changed processes in the management.

However, in solving problems concerning the present and future, the following factors are to be considered during changing process.

(i) *Systematic thinking:* It is the act of seeing patterns in the wholeness, rather than focusing on individual parts manifested in departments and divisions whose functions are counted in functional approaches and quarterly reports etc.

(ii) *Developed capability:* It is not essential that an individual performance gives guarantee to the organizational learning during the course of learning capabilities and developing process.

(iii) *Surfacing and testing models:* These two ingredients are most important tools in consideration of changing process. Because mental models decide thoughts and actions simultaneously for bringing surface to make people aware of their existence and modification of necessity is needed there.

(iv) *Binding shared vision* : The aims and objectives of the organization are to be considered in making of changed process while the process relates with cohesion through building a shared vision rather than relying on formalized systems and procedures. Because the shared vision ensures a deep personal involvement and commitment of members of the organization.

(v) *Team learning:* During the time of changing process, the organization must keep watch on team learning in creation of results and desired an enacting vision in consideration of handling problems concerned with the wing.

Thus, the organizational strategy must give focus on evolved vision, mission, values for the organization, formulae based on macro level. Strategies, structure and policies for the governance of the organization and overall supervision of the management—monitoring, reviewing and reporting on performance—all these factors are highly concerned with ensured optimum utilization and effectiveness of human resources.

Test Questions

1. Discuss the concept of technological innovations.
2. What do you mean by sociotechnical systems? Can better teamwork be achieved through system design?
3. Explain the process of technological innovation.

18

The Organisational Implications of Successful Technological Change

Organisation Structure and Design

Organisation structure is the pattern in which various parts or components are interrelated so it establishes the relationship among various position and activities in the organisation.

Every organisation has a goal and the organisation structure is one of the forces that affects the goal of the organisation and is designed in such a manner as to serve as an instrument to accomplish the social goal. The efficiency with which and the extent to which an organisation is able to achieve its goal, are, to a great extent, determined by its structure. So, a structure is developed to give the shape to as tentative idea thought about at the initial stage. The structure is beginning in very simple because the size of organisation is small and it becomes complex and needs planning and a systematic approach as the organisation expands. At this stage a well planned and designed structure emerges out.

In a large industrial unit, where services of a large number of people are required, there is always a problem of assigning duties and delegating authority in order to achieve the organisation objective.

Organising function primarily deals with the grouping of activities and establishment of authority relationship, among various people working in the organisation. The establishment of authority relationship in a formal organisation is vital for a clear understanding of authority relationship. This relationship integrated different parts of the enterprises into a coordinated whole. It defines the relationship between person and person, department and department and department and person.

Designing of organisation structure is considered to be a matter of choice among a large number of alternatives avilable depending upon the size and the nature of the enterprises yet there are three common forms of organisation structure and these are:

1. Line organisation,
2. Functional organisation, and
3. Line and staff organisation.

A manager can adopt any one of the above three forms of structure which he finds most suitable for his organisation provided he is sufficiently aware of the various alternatives and their pros and cons. We are discussing the above forms of organisation structure with their merits and demerits one by one and some other factors as well.

1. Line Organisation Structure. Line organisation structure is perhaps the oldest and the simplest form of organisation and is also known as scalar, military vertical or departmental organisation. Under this organisation the line of authority flows vertically from top to bottom. There is a single head of the organisation who commands the whole affairs. The chief executive holds the authority and he delegates it to the subordinates and the subordinates further reduces at each successive level down the organisation. In this way, principles of 'unity of command' and the 'scalar chain' are followed in this organisation. It defines the superior subordinate relationship and each one knows from who he is to receive the instruction.

2. Functional Organisation Structure. As the nature suggests, their functional authority relationship, all activities of the organisation are grouped together according to various basic functions such as production, marketing, finance and personnel, etc. And each

A Simple chart of line organisation is given below:

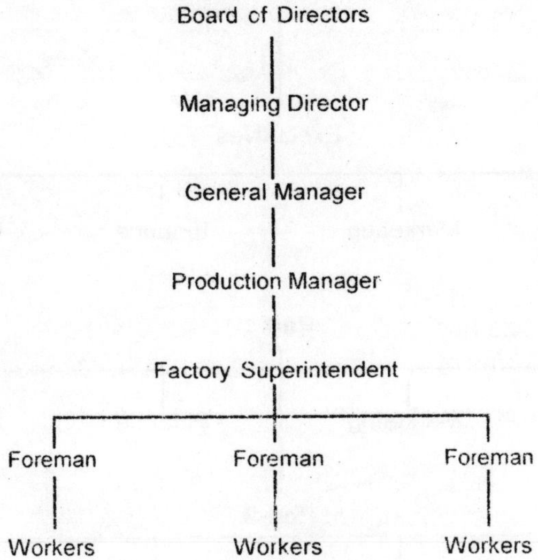

Line Organisation

function is put under the charge of a specialist who is fully responsible for carrying out the function well throughout the organisation. Thus, an individual in this organisation receive instruction from several functional heads in respect of the various activities. The divisional heads report to one specialist with reference to one function, to another for another function and so on, the functional authority relationship can easily be understood by the following chart:

The functional authority relationship was emphasised for the first time by F.W. Talyor's 'functional foremanship'. In fact, the Tylor's functional foremanship's is a pattern of supervision at shop rather than an organisation structure.

3. Line and Staff Organisation Structure

This type of organisation has been evolved to achieve the advantages of the two forms of organisation that we discussed, i.e. line organisation and functional organisation. The first inisists too much on the unity of command while the later too much on decentralization on control. In order to strike a happy balance between the two, the line and staff organisation was evolved.

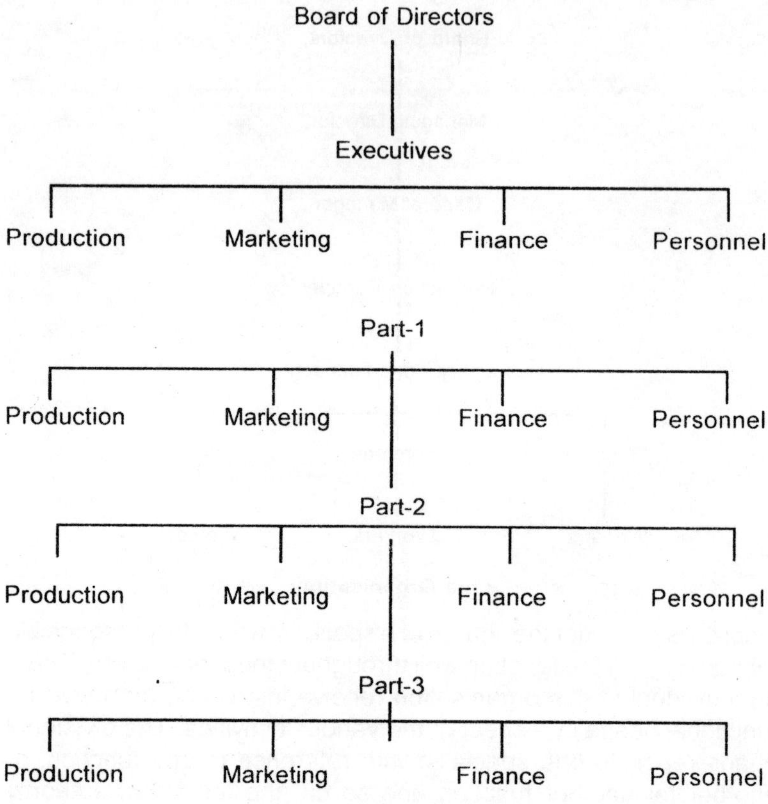

Functional Organisation

In this organisation, the structure is basically that of line organisation but staff officers, who are functional experts are provided to advise the line authorities in the performance of their duties. Staff officer in person or through their staff assistants render advisory aids to the line officers but they have no power to enforce it. The power of enforcement remains with the line officers.

In actual practice, it is sometimes very difficult to determine which position or department is line or staff. Generally group of activities or departments which substantively or directly contribute towards, the organisation's overall objectives is line and those which are indirect in their contribution is staff. Line and staff organisation may be shown in the following figure.

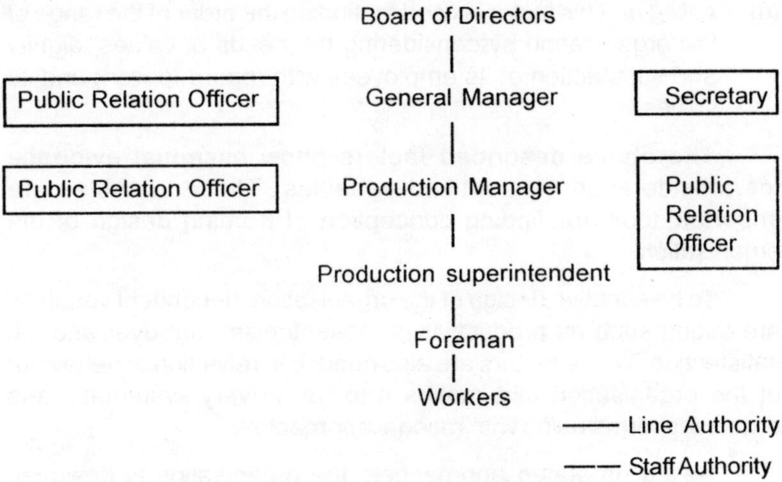

Line and Staff Organisation

Design of Organisation

Any organisation consisting of its members is to function and adhere for achieved goals in forms of goods and services. The behaviour of members is accounted for their assigned duties. Because, duties of persons are identified for causes and effects of the organisation.

The design of any organisation is accounted for creation of uniqueness of rules and turbulent environment that create a model emphasising a relation between persons and management of the organisation. The relation between the two aspects exists into the following sub-classified four categories that are used in filling the model.

(a) *autocratic* : It is indicated for psychologic and maintenance thal depend on power, governed rules and following premium on obedience.

(b) *custodial:* It is indicated for security, and maintenance of men in the organisation in tackling the problems of economic resources,

(c) *supportive*: It is meant for knowing the order of the organisation in forms of leadership participation organisational persons and created environment with better motivation.

(d) *collegial*: This factor is used for finding the order of the range of the organisation by considering the needs of values, dignity and satisfaction of its employees with regard to work and its values.

The above described factors show essential evidence for consideration of identified variables. These variables are important tools for finding conception of framing design of the organisation.

To be effective design of the organisation, dependent variables are taking such as productivities, absenteeism, turnover and job satisfaction. These factors are also needed in reflection of behaviour of the organisation that makes it to run in very systematic and organised forms using with rational approaches.

Based on stated approaches, the organisation is designed to follow systemic modus operandi explained in rational-economic-social and other considerable factors. Because, the design of the organisation is characterised to control over predictable and unpredictable factors emphasising on responses of groups of men involved with the organisation with stricking policies by democratic and consultative manners for existence of effectiveness showing an attribute of "social ethic".

Further, the design of the organisation must bring about rational approaches following systematic assences of administrative thoughts, unbiased and futile goals justifying results in formation of perception, social and economic factors for finding information and creating environment.

This form of organisation is very popular except the very small organisations but staff expert advice becomes necessary at some level.

2. Skill and Labour Demands

It has been tried to find out the exact impact of technological changes upon skill and labour demands. Technological applications are very difficult to categorise.

Therefore, it is the growth and awareness of skill which is important for the workers and the company. It has been practically observed that those organisations which have spent (contributed) more heavily in changing their skill base have prospered most when they want to develop. For example, The Philips India wanted to improve the skill of the workers. For this purpose old restrictions were removed, but every individual was offered the opportunity of constant skill development. The idea was to provide better opportunities for skill development, with the growth of such a culture a long term work force is created which is used for learning. This becomes a norm of the future skill development of the fresh recruits.

When a new technology is adopted it is accompanied by a number of features whereas there is need for employees to work in teams, in case of traditional jobs. The traditional jobs and groups are those where tasks are largely well defined and controlled. There is very little change. In modern developed jobs responsibility for programming, planning, work, organisation of quality is included.

In the modern developed jobs computer control systems would become more and more sophisticated and useful to reduce the technical uncertainty. The environmental dynamics means outside world, like the markets, competitors and changing customer demands. Where they have little impact and the work demands can be predicted, but the traditional jobs are stable. Now the requirements are increasing and changing and require that the organisations should be more flexible and responsive to the needs and demands. One another factor becoming important in all the major economics of the world is that the dropouts of schools are decreasing in number. More children have taken birth and increasing population. The traditional companies are introducing new technology and new manpower in the labour market. They will work in the situation so that there should be retraining.

The population growth requires that the companies have to fulfill the requirement of new products and processes and not to retaining or recruitment. The trend shows that skill will reduce and the organisation will have to provide more interesting and stimulating jobs.

3. Employment Patterns

The technological changes is fast improving which attract the employment pattern for the technologist and those affected by the impact of technology.

The technologists are those who have the understanding of the technology and the skill of its use. But sometimes they feel neglected within the organisation. Therefore, the dashing and frustrated people often start their own organisation.

In an organisation every section have separate planning and objective. Entrepreneurship is different from the routine of the organisation. But this is a disadvantage, because when the technology is transferred from one section to the other, this transfer is not effective because of the big cultural gap. This is challenge to manage the change process. Employment patterns for innovative organisation involvessome form of networking and self-employment.

A successful company needs both good innovators and good operations staff. This is a difficult balance of employment pattern. The need to retain key staff of both types innovators and managers, for whom different patterns may apply. The second consideration is the employment patterns of employees because of technological change. The impact of technological change can be wide and different. It can have its impact on the market forces, new capital investment as well as manpower.

At some places the demand and supply ratio has to be efficient and qualitative for the effective running of the organisation. Another question that comes with this is the limitation which is put before the operations management. Because the company is dependent on only one suppliers. Suggestion schemes can be very effective. They can generate new ideas and introduce changes. There are number of guidelines.

- Give the process a high profile.
- Quick action within a few days.
- Follow them up with individual and his team.
- The head of the team is to be involved.

- Others are to be encouraged to initiate their new and good ideas.
- Quick action to be taken on good ideas.
- Managerial resources are to be provided to any programme of the programme is to drop.

4. Quality Circles

The multifunctional teams manage change. Quality circles are part of managing change these days. The success of this depends upon the will and desire to improve quality.

The important issues are the scope of such teams activity, the support they receive and their scope for implementation. Innovative companies have evolved the concept of quality circles dealing with immediate problems towards creativity teams. To make the idea effective its working must be demonstrated and practiced from top to bottom.

5. Attraction and Selection

The selection of the right person is very difficult. It is difficult to decide as to who is innovative and ready to face the innovative culture. In course of face interview there are chances of selection of different types and aptitudes of people. This has been proved by a number of research studies.

There are some guidelines about the proper selection, training and its success. Innovation is uncertain and risky process it has high potential rewards. Therefore to promote innovation innovative environment is required, where people with different potentialities can get the opportunity to be innovative. In this way individuals will select themselves their choice of job through achievement.

In a study of management practices among high technology companies in Scotland, it has been found that a large number of employers use the analytical testing techniques for selection of different categories of jobs. The idea was to find the aptitude of the candidates towards a particular kind of job. To know their attitude towards cooperation, change work and flexibility and aptitudes for learning and accepting change. By this way such companies encourage and provide opportunities for their employees to adopt culture and environment of the company as a priority. The culture, skill and investment is needed both for immediate needs and for future development.

Majaro has identified some selection criteria and selection ideas for creative managers.

1. *Conceptual fluency*—the ability to generate ideas.
2. *Mental fluency*—the ability to shift from one way of thinking to another.
3. *Originality*—-being above to give creative answers to old questions, looking at issues in very different views.
4. *The ability to suspend judgment*—this is to avoid instant judgments on new ideas, which may be negative. The innovator will reject most of the new ideas and accept only the tested ones.
5. *Impulse acceptance*—Creative people are often impulsive (restless), as new ideas always keep coming in their mind.
6. *A challenging attitude to authority*—Creative people must challenge the existing order.
7. *Tolerance*—sA creative person should be tolerant of others' ideas. In course of discussion and exchange of views new ideas emerge. This may be innovative and helpful for the Company.

There is a range of initiative which can promote innovation and change.

- Top management should be interested for the improvement in ideas at all levels of the organisation.
- The job of the managers can be secured only when they are innovative and make change in the old system.
- Making creativity and innovation a key performance measure through appraisal and performance management systems.
- The scheme of reward, promotion and developing those people who promote change.

6. Pay Structure and Pay Design

Most often it is found that the pay objectives do not match with the business objectives. In western countries there is no category-wise distribution of pay but on the basis of individual contribution. An innovative and successful individual deserves award and encouragement. But at the same time it is difficult to measure an individual's contribution. Because it is a team work which may lead to success over a long period of time. Short term measures based on individual activity will discourage innovation. Therefore the short term measures are not helpful for the company. The pay-system has also to be long term keeping in view the future prospect of the company.

It is clear from many studies that for technologists more important that money is the opportunity to develop their ideas with the necessary support and help. But if both the facilities are available at the same time, then it is certainly a successful business for the company.

7. Participation of Employee

Commitment and involvement of the employees for the company is very significant for competitive advantage.

In the stratified top company there are few aspects of the business which are open to challenge. But no such challenge by the senior executive. Because they have been engaged in performance and productivity. More important thing is for them to read the market demand to make change and opportunity accordingly. Hence, the employee involvement in this context can be more useful. Then the focus of the objective can shift from only problem solving to creative teams to make opportunities for the future. A writer Tom Peter in his book *Thriving On Chaos* beautifully presented an example, by drawing the figure of a boat representing the organisation and a waterline showing the areas of the organisation open to creativity and change. For organisation with a high water line there are few aspects of the business which are open to challenge except by the most senior executives. In this type of organisation people are told to stick to their jobs and not to interfere in other people's work and activity. On the other hand organisation with low water line where challenge and debate are valued, the only thing unchallengeable is the purpose of the business itself.

This openness and challenge is a stroke to management on their position of power and control to influence their organisation. In this situation employee involvement becomes both real and difficult to handle. Because the employee involvement which is truly creative will pose a threat to those who are in power.

The challenge most often comes when employee involvement is invited through one of many mechanisms, such as quality circles, problem solving groups and suggestion schemes. But how such activities are handled is important for development and innovation.

8. Suggestion Schemes

Suggestion Scheme is one of the low priority areas of the companies. Most companies put on the wall a letter box, written on it - suggestion. But the process has become ineffective and neglected, due to a number of factors.

Suggestion schemes can be very effective. There are a number of guidelines—

- Give the process a high profile;
- Give quick feed back, i.e., within days of submission;
- Take ideas seriously;
- Follow them up with the individual and with their team;
- Involve the work team's boss;
- Praise the initiative, whatever be the quality of the idea;
- Demonstrate quick action on good idea;
- Allocate managerial resources to the programme or drop it.

9. Patterns of People

It is a matter of particular concern that to some extent people system obstruct innovation within organisations. For example,the pay system, the way the organisation communicates and how it recruits etc. The personnel profession develops on the basis of a set of systems and procedures, which bring consistency, order and conformity to an organisation.

Impact of Technology on Trade Union

The first post-war trade union interest was seen during the early 1960s. The impact of which was automation on working people

The first post-war trade union interest was seen during the early 1960s. The impact of which was automation on working people and their trade unions. There were apprehensions that because of more mechanization, jobs would be cut in the manufacturing sector. But no such crisis was observed. Again with the introduction of electronics during late 1970s and early 1980s the trade union felt that it would be major cause of job reduction. This fear and economic stagnation gave a pressure to maintain jobs and emphasis was placed upon 'new technology agreements'. These were considered to be a means by which the introduction of technological change would be negotiated or jointly decided upon between trade unions and management. These agreements provided communications and consultative structure which helped in bringing the desired change.

The new technology proved ineffective because of several reasons. It should be concerned either with trade unions or management in solving the problems of job reduction, job security, pay, retraining and flexibility.

Without any job security the people can not be helpful for giving suggestions for improvement.

Moreover the power of the trade union varies and depends on a number of factors. There may be the interests of the employees related with the introduction of the advanced level technology and so on.

The challenging question for the managers are:

- Who is responsible for managing the organisational implications for technological change in your organisation?
- Upto what extent these are relevant and useful for your organisation.
- How much your technologists are aware of these implications?
- Does your corporate strategy recognise the impact it has on technological innovation and investment?

In finding conclusion of given study, there is found the most crucial challenge to industrial/business organisations to motivate human behaviour towards higher productivity and greater work efficiency. These two factors are most important in respect of satisfying organisational climate for achieving goals in different types

The organisational climate refers to external and internal environmental conditions in which the organisation exists and grows for achievements of goals to the people. The external factors indicate various factors such as (a) cultural / social system, (b) science and technology systems.

Though, in India the upsurge in industrial activity requires a thorough evaluation of our approach for better considerations of technologies. For intense, in agricultural sectors, there would be better optimization of input resources like seed soil conditioning, fertilizer-micronutrient mixes, pesticides and so on necessitating changes in overall agricultural management. The management provides the potential areas of employment laid on value added agro-food industry. Also the potentiality is credited in fields of cereals, milk, fruits, vegetables and horticulture, floriculture, mushroom cultivation, etc., which create extended form of employment opportunities. The opportunity is laid in absorption of large number of persons in the field of agro-food industries/business around the sector.

In the industrial and manufacturing sector the use of modern electronic and hi-tech gadgets are continual features in terms of resurgence of engineering industries, machine tools, foundry, electrical machinery and transport equipment alienated with industrial/ business organisations. Moreover, India is an important world in leading software for manufacturing to acquire rapid re-orientation in the coming millennium for inducing new technologies that are introduced in the economy. The rapid industrialization absorbs only a fraction of unemployed youth.

Thus, the increasing interconnectivity across sectors like structure and manufacturing has spurred the demand for services directly related to such sectors—usually known as focus area for development. Hence, with substantial truth, India emerges as a global leader in the services sector with its vast and skilled human resources being its core strength. The services are accounted for trade, storage, transport and communication and finance where all they are counted for the following:

(1) total review of the skill;

(2) development system for better match between demand and supply;

(3) identification of thrust areas; and

(4) creation of new demands in sectors like manufacture—telecom, power, roads, posts, media or infotech by means of technological changes in the organisation.

Thus, technological changes have brought scenario of sustained growth of GDP, economic and social infrastructure for building competence in the sector for implementation of maximum benefits.

In these regards, an explanation may be given for vision of the new millennium comprising of social and economic empowerment of the human being that would lead economic prosperity in realization of new vision. The vision justifies organisational climate showing influences on job involvement which is a necessary condition. The condition stresses on level of aspirations and the degree of internationalisation of the organization affecting the job involvement of the employee in different sectors such as managerial policy and its practice, personal policy and its practice, standard performance, and competency showing the result of recognition and reward etc. Further, the technological changes identify the highest impact on the measures of organisational performance and stepwise forward regression is performed there.

In addition to, the impact of technological changes on the organisations is understood for its culture comprising of (a) a pattern of basic assumptions, (b) invention, discovery and development followed by a given group, (c) learning in order to cope with its problem of external adaptation and internal integration, (d) working conditions in valid forms, and (e) correct way to perceive, think and feel in relation to complex problem for the new entrants to the organisation with strong belief, considerable effort and definite desire. Because the effectiveness of the organisation has been defined as the ability of organisation to mobilize its center of power for action, production and adaptation following positive responses for achieving orientation in forming participative culture.

Thus, the technological changes bring greater impact on the organisation with adoption of elements of review, reflect redirect, reorient, renew human resources in it through a continuous process of individual and collective developmental initiatives for a closed step to organisation effectiveness linked with instruments, processes and outcomes in dealing with job challenge, freedom of action, delegation, responsibility and planning in standard forms.

Test Questions

1. How much the technologists are associated to these implications?
2. Explain about those responsible for managing the organisational implications of technological changes.
3. Whether our corporate strategy identifies the impact it has on technological innovation as well as investment.

19

Performance/Potential Evaluation in the Context of New Technology

The object of an organisation is to give qualitative performance. The performance should be scheduled to follow effective management forming technological process. The technological considerations cover integrated approaches of cultural climate followed by limited conditions. But such induction is used for high need achievement to individuals to maximize their gains at the cost of group's achievement, harmony and quality of relationship as suggested by J.B.P. Sinha (1968) in his contribution work culture in the Indian context, New Delhi.

Thus, in India there is highly concerned activities of technological advances in view of personalized relationship, affiliation, paternalism and dependency. That measure to say the social-cultural relationship between leaders and subordinates along with the contingency, approach, reinforcement principle, and the quality of dyadic exchange to develop a dynamic and growth oriented model of leadership. These relationships are found more promising to define work culture of organisations as more effective and creative in national wealth significantly to solve complex problems of the society.

It is the process of obtaining, analysing and recording information about the relative worth of an employee. Although Performance Appraisal and Potential Evaluation are used synonymously, but Performance Appraisal is a wider term than Potential Evaluation. The Potential Evaluation evaluates the different traits of the employee by comparing the qualitative factors such as nature of individual, physical and mental ability etc. Whereas Performance Appraisal evaluates the performance of an employee by quantitative factors such as quantity of output and rejected output, standard of work, etc.

Thus, in Potential Evaluation the stress is on 'what he is' While in Performance Appraisal, the emphasis is on 'what he does' and 'what potentiality does he posses'?

Performance Appraisal : Performance Appraisal is a systematic, periodic and so far as humanly possible, an impartial rating of employee's excellence in matters pertaining to his present job and to his potentialities for a better job — Flippo.

Potential Evaluation : Potential Evaluation attempt to systematic, periodic and, so far as humanly possible, an impartial rating of an employee's excellence in matters pertaining to his present job and to his potentialities for a job. — Edwin, B. Flippo.

Purposes of Performance Appraisal :

- to improve job performance and identify the potentialities for other work.
- to identify the need and areas for further training of the employees.
- to assist in determining promotion and transfer policies.
- to reduce the grievances among the employees.
- to make the compensation plans more scientific and rational.
- to help in proper placement of the workers after the completion of their training.
- to facilitate research in personnel management.
- to develop positive relations in between superior and subordinate.

Q. What is appraisal? How appraisal is to be implemented?

1. Appraisal is a two way discussion between the appraisor and the appraisee.
2. It is an open document that both appraisor and the appraisee agrees and sign.
3. It is a plan for future.
4. It is a constructive criticism of the performance and personality of the appraisee in the immediate past.
5. It's meeting without emotions being involved.

The traditional methods focus more on the trait of an employee than on his job performance criteria of standards, the personal bias of subjectivity of the evaluator affects the ratings.

One study of appraisal in General Electric Co., USA revealed that the traditional approach to performance appraisal caused the following responses:

(a) The very nature of the appraisal system led to criticism.

(b) Criticism exercised a negative impact of goal attainment.

(c) Criticism increased antagonism and defensiveness among employees resulting in inferior performance.

(d) Praise had little effect one way of the other.

The traditional systems of appraisal are based on judgment role of the supervisor. In order to overcome these weaknesses some new techniques of performance appraisal have been developed. These techniques are described below:

Modern Methods

It is important in the context of new technology for quality development.

Assessment Centre Method. All Assessment Centre method is a multiple assessment of several individuals performed simultaneously by a group of trained evaluators using a variety of group and individual exercises. Typically individuals from different departments are brought together to spend two or three days working on individual or group assignment similar to ones they will be handling if they are promoted.

Evaluators evaluates, deserve and rank the performance of all the participants both collectively and individually by using simultation techniques computer simulation method, business games, case studies and in-basket exercises.

Now let us see how these techniques are helpful in our potential development.

(a) *Computer Simulation Method* : The computer permits training, in which the trainee interacts directly with the computer programme for exp. the trainee can read question directly from the computer screen, supply the answer via the keyboard, and immediately receive a grade of corrected answer. This immediate feed-back can be quite beneficial, especially if the trainee must master one unit of material before procedure to new materials.

(b) *Gaming Simulation or Mgt. Games* : These are mgt. development exercises in which participants are given background information instruction about rules and condition and perhaps roles to play. One example would be complex computerized games which are frequently played on an electronic computer that has been programmed for a particular game. In such a game, each team makes decisions on various matters such as fixation of price, level of production, inventory level, and so forth. Since each team is competing with others, each firm's decisions will affect the results of all others. All the firm's decisions are fed into a computer which is programmed to behave somewhat like a real market. The computer provides the results, and the winner is the team which has accumulated largest profit. In the light of such results, strength and weaknesses of decisions are analysed. Another example (not computerized) is a consensus exercise in which members of group make individual decisions and then attempt to improve their individual scores through effective group interaction. The trainees are divided into groups or different teams. Each has to discuss and arrive at decisions concerning such subjects as production, pricing, research expenditure, advertising etc. assuming itself to be the mgt. group of a simulated or approximate firm.

(c) *Role Playing* : Its purpose is to increase the trainee's skill in dealing with other people. One of its greatest use in connection with human relations training, but it is also used in sales training as well. It is spontaneous acting of a realistic situation involving two or more persons under class-room situations. It is a method of human interaction which involve, stage play of realistic behaviour in an imaginary of hypothetical situation. Participants are typically provided with a specific situation which they must analyse, and then each participant assumes and acts out the role of specific person. Role-playing has many advantages. By this method, a trainee can broaden his experience by trying different approaches, while in actual situation, he often has only one chance.

(d) *Films and TV Shows* : These are also useful technique for training. It is an effective techniques of transmitting information and of enriching the knowledge of trainees. 'They generate interest among trainees by dramatizing usually specific events, incidents and realities. These technique can be used by other approaches like lectures and conference to brush up trainees.

The other teams assume themselves, competitor and react to the decision. This immediate feed-back helps to know the relative performance of each team.

(c) *Case Studies or Case Discussions* : A case is a written account of a trained reporter of analyst seeking to describe an actual situation. Some cases are merely illustrative, others are detailed and comprehensive demanding extensive and intensive analytical ability. Cases are widely used in a variety of programmes. Cases are prepared on the basis of actual experiences of organisations, i.e., actual business situations that happened in various organisations. Case studies involve providing the trainees with written or video taped descriptions of decision making situation or cases. The participants are required to analyse each case and make appropriate decisions.

(f) *In Basket Exercise* : The trainee is given background information about a simulated company, its products, key personnel, various memos, letters, requests, and all data pertaining to the firm that a manager might find in the in basket upon arriving at work. The trainee has to understand all this, make notes, delegate tasks, and prepare memos within a specified amount of time. In basket exercise develops various kinds of abolition in the trainee such as (i) situational judgement in being able to recall details, establish prioritie, interrelate items, and determine need for more information, (ii) Willingness to make decision and take action. (iii) Good time mgt. which is important enough in most managerial jobs.

(g) *360 Degree Feed-Back* : The idea of upward feed-back developed by firms are called 360 Degree of Feed-Back. In this an employee's performance information is collected "all round" that is from his supervisors, subordinates, peers and internal or external customers. This feed-back is very useful for training and development. The computerized system compile or collect at this feed-back information and facts into individualized reports that are prepared and presented to the person being rated, which becomes useful for the ratees to meet their own supervisors and sometimes with their subordinates to share the information what they deserve is essential for the purpose of skill building.

Behaviourally Anchored Rating Scale (BARS)

It is designed to identify the job's critical areas of performance and to describe behaviour of the job which is more effective and less effective for getting results. Performance is evaluated by asking the rater to record specific and observable job behaviour of an employee and then to compare these observations with a "behaviourally anchored rating scale". As a result the supervisor is in a position to compare the employee's actual behaviour with behaviour that has been previously determined to more or less effective.

BARS method has several advantages. First, the ratings are likely to be accurate because these are done by experts. Secondly, the method is more reliable and valid as it is job specific and identifies observable and measurable behaviour. The rater's bias is reduced. Systematic clustering of critical incidents helps in making the dimensions independent of one another. Thirdly, ratings are likely to be more acceptable due to employee participation.

BARS method, has several disadvantages: First it is very time consuming and expensive to develop BARS for every job. Secondly, behaviours used are more activity-oriented than results-oriented.

Appraisal by Results (MBO)

Result oriented appraisal is the outcome of the modern management technique known as management by objectives (MBO). MBO has been described as a philosophy of management which seeks to minimize external controls and maximize internal motivation through joint goal setting between the manager and the subordinate and increasing the subordinate's own control of his work.

'Management by objectives can be described as a process whereby the superior and subordinate managers of an organisation jointly identify its common goals, define each individuals major areas or responsibility in terms of results expected of him and use these measures as guides for operating the unit and assessing the contribution of each of its members.

These are the engaging steps inperformance evaluation through which MBO are to be listed in quick succession.

(1) *Set Organisation Objectives* : First, all objectives of the organisation in conspicuous as of performance are laid down. The objectives are to be defined in lucid, precise and measurable terms. They should be challenging yet approachable. An in depth evaluation of internal environment and external environment of the organisation is made to set these objectives.

(2) *Defining Process Targets* : On the score of organisational goals performance norms for each and every employees may be decided on the ground of organisation charts and job description. Every subordinate write down his own performance objectives which are coupled with work, and job orientation. His manager also writes down the goals he thinks the subordinate should strive for. 'The two then embark upon the discussion reach an agreement and put the agreed goals in writing. Thus employees are dynamically engrossed in goal setting. Clear attainable goals help canalize energies in the healthy direction. And the employee should be acquainted with the basis on which he would be appraised. These goals are periodically revived and revived to keep them flexible and updated.

The level of performance is satisfactory enough to notch up the goal defined lucidly and clearly. Measure check point are established to fathom progress towards the goals. Action plans needed to attain the goals are decided through mutual consultation among an employee and his superior. Joint goal setting and joint action planning are the important ingredients of appraisal through MBO.

(3) *Performance Reviews* : Recurrent performance meetings between the manager and the subordinate should be held. Monthly review may be used and then extended to quarterly reviews. In the review meetings, there is an assessment of weaknesses and constraints identified and step to be initiated to streamline the performance to be decided. Subordinate take part in the process in an active manner. This paves way to self-control by the employee.

(4) *Evaluation* : After every performance review feedback or performance is conveyed to the employee so that he can regulate and improve on his own performance on the score of performance. Review rewards are also decided. Novel goals and performance targets are decided for the next period.

Test Questions

1. Distinguish between performance appraisal and potential evaluation through modern methods.
2. Describe the process of performance appraisal through modern methods.
3. How can performance appraisal be made more effective? Discuss.
4. Explain the essentials of an effective performance appraisal system.
5. Write notes on-

   (a) Assessment Centre.

   (b) Behaviourally Anchored Rating Scales.

   (c) Appraisal by Results or MBOs.

20
Career Development, Self-Development and Managemant Development

Career Development

This study makes an exploration of the systematic study for guiding principles of human resources. They have been undertaken into consideration of different achieved position laid on individual or collective career path.

Undoubtedly, various writers like David Decenzo & Stephen Robbens proposed a five stage model that has been generalised. Such generalisation occurs to most do the people during their adult years regardless of the type of work. The following explanations may be undertaken for five stages model career.

Exploration - It is the factor convinced for preemployment stage. It is widely used for upto 25 yrs which has been considered for schooling period unformally known transitional period. During this period individual enter into their choosen career with their forceful activities. Their entrance shows parents, teachers, friends, relatives and some other's decision and advice. This exploration period gives a number of expectations. Their expectations may be cropped or not.

Establishment - This is the several factor used for individuals career ranging from the age of 25-35 years. It establishes the search of work. It wants real world. It shows to learn any thing by gradual means with increased responsibility. Such gradual increment of knowledge begins with uncertainties and anxieties.

Mid Career - It considers the age of individuals ranging from 35-50 years. During this period most people feel their career in doldrum. They do not make an assessment a correct path of their making career. Sometimes they are learner and sometimes they are novice. A lot of mistake are being made by them. This state is highly complexed and critical to the individuals because he is not in a position to take decision with correct estimate for enlighting his goals. Thus, he is found in transitional form with greater responsibilities.

Large Career - It is fourth stage of any individual for making his career ranging from 50-70 years of his age. This period is found in continution to grow through the mid career stage. This period shows for the individual acceptance of luxury relax and to enjoy through various means. The means may be described as mobility based an knowledge and experience. This period makes considerable forwardness towards retirement for opportunities but this doesn't show sufficient proofs for consideration of making career of the individual.

Decline - This is the last factor involved in the individuals career ranging from to 70 and above. It is stepping towards difficulty to almost every individual. It is very highlighted and major component for making an identification of individual. It doesn't give any breadth on increment in the career of individual rather it becomes hardest and toughest following seriousness. Because the individuals become free for such stage. They don't want to take responsibility if they desire for making the responsibilities they are meant for few and less structured.

Organisational Career Development

For measuring of development of given subject the following measures have been assumed. These measures have been treated as latest tools for developing career of superiors & subordinates of any organisation.

1. *Career Counselling*: This is the process for processing the guiding principles in making career development programme. Undoubtedly, to any organisational set up there requires performance – a sort of appraisal or review it review following

award or punishment to the subordinates through their respective superiors. Thus, we can say that element of activities of subordinates are being counted at every moment during their discharge of their duties, particularly production process. This process requires following elements which might be existed as employees aspects. It provide goals aspiration, expectations towards employees of organisation. These factors involve to such specific element which ranges for the next five years or longer to make career of the employees.

(i) *Managerial aspects* : This aspects is another element. It approaches optimistic views with high degree of level of aspirations with realistic approaches. The continuation of approaches are more upgraded and make an apportune.

(ii) *Self development in Future Process* : This the third elements for organisational setup in identifying the self development, counted for future in respect of finding new opportunities.

(iii) *Need for essential effort* : This is fourth element for identifying the organisational career development in form of new developmental activities or assigning new jobs. This is needed for employees career for further growth for the organisation. Thus, the mentioned elements are more fruitful for making the career development particularly stressing the realistic approaches aspiration for both exhaling and inhaling. The term exhaling is connotated here towards the superior of the organisation where "inhaling" compounding for employees of the organisation.

For career counselling the following objects might be taken into consideration such as provision of guidance, advice to employee understanding of anything in clear form, immediate responses towards the employees to understand the forces in dynamic achievement for creating an operation of environment. The environment must be achieved with personal satisfaction and pleasure of responsibilities because they are mainly developed stages for considerable changes in career development for both superior and subordinates of the organisation. This process would be tackled by the counselling measures. It stimulates aspirations in two sided forms that gives actions and interactions of exhanging of thoughts between two bodies (superior and subordinates).

2. *Initial jobs . This element to the development of organisational career provi*des an establishment of degree of stimulation. It is

significantly related with career success. It is retained in their organisation with initial challenges. It is continued ranging from subsequent year. It is useful in case of recruitment and selection of right kind of people for the organisation. It gives significant advantages to both organisations and individuals of the society in making career building.

3. *Information relating to career option.* This element show an attribute of information which must be substantive that means the awaited informations not to be followed with successful and relevant informations for creating healthy and realiable data following a good possesses in environmental scenario.
4. *Information relating to jobs.* It provides full information indicating human resources. The resources must be adhered to practice for provisions of jobs. The jobs are available and required for promoting achievements. But such function is involved in managerial's assignment because it is the duty of manager of every organisation to assign any jobs posting, transfers of an employee with view of challenging his performance.
5. *Workshop Career.* This factor is also important. Its importance is laid due to resource of development in groups. The groups meant provide opportunity for making career particularly retirement of the employee. Because the phase of the retirement deals with frustation over unfulfilled career goals in coping to the interest of the younger.
6. *Assessment Centre.* This is also a factor which might be assessed for career development tools. It feed back for the assessee. It gives a good learning to the individual behaviours domain with awareness.
7. *Changed jobs in periodic form.* There is no doubt that a man becomes monotonous in continuation of one job. The job must have dynamic feature. There must be avenues for making development phase to phase. Without such implication of phase, it is not possible to make career development to any individual of the organisation. Thus, this factor gives a potent element in providing relevant information to management with regard to employee's approaches.
8. *Sabatical.* This term is used in organisational structure. It denotes for leaves of absence with pay. It is extended for leaves of absence during which the employee does not do this ordinary job such as travel, studies etc. In such case the employees get usual

pay for one year leave after completing seven year service in his service career.

9. *Continuous Education and Training.* This factors encourages employees for continuation of their education and training for making their career for their organisational system. This factor gives more importance with careful aligned aspiration and effective career development programme during the time of job training. Because job training the process for finding offer educational skill course by personal with their organisation.

Individual Career Development

It makes an assessment for self to the individual. It provides better approaches in planning of the career of the individual with seriousness and making an identification of their needs, values and personal goals. But such assessment shows the process of the following : identifying, converting and testing. The first give identification of an organisation with greater skill ranked with interest following related works their respective values. The second factor gives convertion of inventories into general career factors and specific job goals – a limited set of occupation of interest. The third factor stresses a possibilities against the realities of the organisation or job market with personal specialities, high skilled knowledge, action and interaction in providing the reliable feedback concerned with self assessment and opportunities in consequence of finding extended form of interest to the employees.

Self is something of which we are immediately aware. Development is a planned, systematic and continuous process of learning and growth designed to induce behavioural change in individuals by cultivating their mental abilities and inherent qualities through the acquisition, understanding the use for new knowledge insight and skills. Development is designed to include behavioral changes in the executives by cultivating executives talents and knowledge. At development is a self-development and the organisations can only provide for the conditions for the development.

Self-development is an important concept of development of executives of the organisations. Every development is a self-development. Every development starts from self-development.

Self-development has three major elements, the desire to improve matured actions and proper time towards improvement.

Concepts of Self

The forms of self development are:

Basic self-concept. Many self-concepts are developed at different times and in different ways forming a hierarchy in which the basic self concept isshaped by person's social experience at home. These concepts start from home and after sometime by greater environment to make happy and well-adjusted to an executive. Basic self concept includes perception, the role and status in life, values, beliefs and aspirations.

Situational Self-Concept. It depends on the sittuation in which the individual is placed.

Social Self-Concept.Social self means how other perceive you and how you perceive others.

Ideal Self-Concept.What an individual aspires to be and believes what he ought to be.

Development of self-concept and emerging ideas about the self are shaped by interacting with other people. The self-concept is really a social concept and other people are the standards against which the emerging self is measured and defined.

Self-Behaviour. Self behaviour is a very important thing. Behavious may be defined as actions, activities, verbal perception, sometimes, it is caused, and sometimes it is autonomous. His behaviour may be positive or negative but it is always expected that continuous efforts should be made to improve the self-behaviour in changing business environment.

Defensive Behaviour—Defensive Behaviour is an example of negative response. Being a social animal, when on interacts with others, there may be two possibilities either to accept or reject, the result of interaction. If he accepts, means he is flexible and may be experiencing with new behaviour. The person who rejects the response, he cannot experience a new Behaviour, thus he cannot learn much.

Stages of Self-Development

The process of self-development which starts from childhood and ends with the old life can be classified into stages.

Early Childhood. Its life periods are from 0-6 years. During this stage, he learns the self-concept and learns to be a member of the family. He also learns his physical and social realities and tries to learn personal care.

Late Childhood. The period of late childhood is from 6-12 years. During this period, a child develops his habits, tastes, liking or disliking. Also some developmental processes take place during this period like mental development, physical development, social development, emotional development, and speech development. Teacher-parents should create such environment where he accepted, loved and recognized. Teachers should make them understand the meaning and reasons of punishment and should also show sympathetic attitude towards them. So that he could follow discipline and will try to be disciplined from his core of heart.

Adolescence. A period from 12 to 18 years. During this stage, he develops a sense of identity and self-confidence. It is the period of rapid growth or revolutionary changes of life, i.e., social, physical, emotional and mental.

This stage of maturation of reproduction process varies from individual to individual, from sex to sex. It also depends on climatic conditions children of hot countries grow to adolescence quickly than those of cold countries. In this stage people find very difficult in adjusting with themselves, with family and with the society at large.

Adulthood. This covers a wide range of varieties of human life beginning from 18 years to and above upto the renewal or resignation. This phase is most important for an executive.

Management Development

Management development (also known as employee development or executive development), often referred to as human resource development (HRD), is about the provision of learning, team and organizational performance.

Management or executive development is a systematic process of growth and development by which managers develop their abilities to manage. In fact, it is a process of learning by which executives gain or increase their knowledge, skills, insights and attitude to effectively deal with the environment of the organisation. It is more future-oriented and more concerned with education than is employee training.

Edwin Flippo. "Management development includes the process by which managers and executives acquire not only skills and competency in their present jobs but also capabilities for future managerial task increasing difficulty and scope."

Characteristics of Management Development

Education process : Management development is predominantly an education process rather than training process. Successful managers have specialised skills to think and understand.

Business oriented process : The business determines what kind of managers it requires to accomplish its strategic goals, as well as how to obtain and develop such managers.

Unending process : Management development is unending exercise that never ends. It continues throughout and executive's entire professional career because learning and education have no limits.

Long-term process : Managerial skills cannot be developed overnight. Skills have to be continuously refreshed and sharpened alongwith the changes taking place due to technological, social, legal, economic, and political advancements.

Betterment of knowledge and skills : Management development results for the betterment of individual's knowledge, skills, insights to accomplish organizational goals.

Objective of Management Development

- To improve the performance of managers at all levels to expose managers to the latest concept and techniques.
- To impart basic knowledge and skills to the new managers.
- To ensure management succession within the organization to build up a second line of competent managers and prepare them to occupy more responsible position as and when needed.
- To broaden the minds and thinking of senior managers. By providing senior managers opportunities for interchange of experience within and outside to correct arrowness of outlook.
- To impart customer education effective dealing with customers.

Methods or Techniques of Management Development

The methods or techniques of management development can be divided in two categories: (A) On-the-job techniques, and (B) Off-the-Job techniques.

(A) On-the-job Techniques or Approaches of Management Development. Some of the popular on-the-job techniques are discussed below:

1. *Coaching* : Under coaching method the employee is trained by his superior. It involves direct personnel instruction and guidance, usually with extensive demonstrations and

continuous critical evaluation and correction.

2. *Positional Rotation* : The trainee is periodically related from job to job instead of sticking to one job so that he may acquire a general background of different jobs.
3. *Understudy* : Under this method a superior gives training to a subordinate as his understudy. The purpose of understudy is to prepare someone to fill the vacancy caused by death, retirement, promotion or transfer of the superior.
4. *Committee Assignments* : Assignment to a committee can provide an opportunity for the employee to share in managerial decision making. Committees are in this context may be of two types. When committees are of an "ad hoc" or temporary nature, they often take on task force activities designed to thoroughly go into particular problem, to ascertain alternate solutions and to make recommendations for implementing a solution.
5. *Multiple Management* : Under this technique, a junior-board of young executives is constituted. Major problems are assigned to the junior-board for proper analysis. The board discusses such problems form all angles and in all responsible details, and makes its recommendations to the board of Directors, on the basis of which the Director take decisions.
6. *Project Assignments* : This structure is created when management decided to focus a great amount of talent and resources for a given period on a specific project. Under the project assignment method, a number of trainee executives are put together to work on a project directly related to their functional areas.
7. *Delegation* : Delegation is a powerful training tool at all level when juniors are delegated authority, they learn how to handle it alongwith responsibility. They also learn how to achieve results in the context of delegated authority and responsibility.

(B) Off-the-job Technique or Approaches or Approaches of Management Development

Off- the -job means the training which is imparted away from the work place. The training may be imparted at the company class room or places which are owned by the company, school, colleges, Universities or associations which have no connection with the company's real work place. There are a lot of management development techniques in which executives can take part off-the-job. The more popular and important off-the-job techniques are

(i) *Lectures* : Lectures are of vital important when specialized knowledge regarding facts, principles, theories, concepts, attitude and problem solving abilities are to be taught. Lectures are delivered by specialized trainers or from a superior on the specific topics. The Lecture method is very useful for the organization.

(ii) *Conferences* : In this training system the individuals confer to discuss the issues of common interest to each other. It is a formal and participative meeting, conducted according to organised plan, in which leader seeks to develop knowledge and understanding by obtaining considerable amount of oral participation of the trainees. It lays emphasis on active participation of the members involved. Through this method, earning is facilitated by building up the ideas contributed by confers.

Conference is of three types (i) Direct Discussions in which trainer guides the discussion in such a way that the facts, principles, or concepts are explained. (ii) Second is training conference, the instructor gets the group to pool knowledge and past experience and brings different opinions for particular problems. (iii) It is a seminar in which the trainer or leader defines the problem, encourages and ensures full participation of the conferees.

(iii) *T-Group Training* : It is called popularly as T-Group where T-Stands for technical. This method is usually comprised of association, audio-visual aid and planned reading programmers. Members of this type of training programme are interested to receive new techniques and ideas pertaining to their own vocations. This can only be possible when there is regular supply of profession journals and informal social contacts or gathering and members are kept inform of the latest development in their particular field. To make this type of training a success, audio-video aids, records, tapes and films are generally used in conjunction with other conventional teaching methods. Two things are most required things, i.e., planned and supervised reading and technical publication and the latest journals kept in the library for the use of trainees.

(iv) *Laboratory Training.* Laboratory Training may be described as experience-based learning workshops which utilize one or more approaches, such as case study, role plays, computer simulations, management games or problem-solving exercises, relatively unstructured group discussions etc. Some important Laboratory Training technique may be outlined as follows :

(a) *Simulation models* : The trainee experiences a feeling that he is actually encountering all those conditions. Then he is asked to assumed a particular role in the circumstance and solve the problems by making a decision. He is immediately given a feedback of his performance. There are several important approaches of simulations that can provide that trainees with practice in making managerial decisions, which may be outlined as mentioned below:

(a) *Computer Simulation method :* The computer permits training in which the trainee interacts directly to the computer program, for example, the trainee can read questions directly from the computer screen, supply the answer via keyboard and immediately receive a grade or a corrected answer. This immediate feedback can be quite beneficial specially if the trainee must master one unit of material before procedure to new materials.

(b) *Gaming simulation or Management Games* : These are management development exercises in which participants are given background informations instructions about rules and conditions and perhaps roles to play. One example would be complex computerized games which are frequently played on an electronic computer that has been programmed for a particular game. In such a game, each team makes decisions on various matters such as fixation of price, level of production, inventory level, and so forth. Since each team is competing with others each firm's decisions will affect the results of all others. All the firm's decisions are fed into a computer which is programmed to behave somewhat I like a real market. The computer provides the results, and the winner is the team which has accumulated largest profit. In the light of such results, strength and weaknesses of decisions are analysed. Another example (not computerised) is a consensus exercise in which members of group make individual decisions and then attempt to improve *their individual scores through effective group interaction*. The trainees are divided into groups or different teams. Each has to discuss and arrive at decisions concerning such subjects as production, pricing, research expenditure, advertising etc. assuming itself to be the management group of a simulated or approximate firm.

(c) *Role Playing* : Its purpose is to increase the trainee's skill in dealing with other people. One of its greatest uses in connection with human relations training, but it is also used in sales training as well. It is spontaneous acting of a realistic situation involving two or more persons under class-room situations. It is a method of human interaction which involve, stage play or realistic behaviour in an imaginary or hypothetical situation. Participants are typically provided with a specific situation which they must analyse, and then each participant assumes and acts the role of a specific person. Role playing has many advantages. By this method, a traineee can broaden his experience by trying out different approaches, while in actual situation, he often has only one chance.

(d) *Films and TV Shows* : These are also useful technique for training. It is an effective technique of transmitting the information and of enriching the knowledge of trainees. They generate interest among trainees by dramatizing usually specific events, incidents and realities. These techniques can be used by other approaches like lectures and conferences to brush up trainees.

(e) *Case studies or case discussions* : Cases are prepared on the basis of actual experiences of the organization (i.e., actual business situations that happened in various organizations). Case study involve providing the trainees with written or videotape descriptions of decision-making situations or cases. The participants are required to analyse each case and make appropriate decisions. The case is subsequently discussed, with emphasis normally on the trainees analyses decisions, implication of those decisions and probable decision out-comes.

For example, Executive MBA programmes are often based on this method. Harward Graduate School of Business has popularized this case study analysis approach.

(v) *Transaction Analysis (TA) or Interpersonal Behaviour Analysis* : It is an analysis of communication which is two way and in various forms. It is an intellect tool to understand the basis of behaviour and feeing and it gives people a relational method for analysis and understanding behaviour (of ourselves and otherselves to whom interacting).

There are various selves within each person and these various selves transacted with other people in different ways and these be analysed.

With T.A. people can become more aware than themselves the structure of the individual personality and how they interact with others. It facilitates communication, increases personal effectiveness and help to solve organizational and personal profit, every individual according to T.A. theory has three ego States which are separate and distinct source of behaviour

(i) Parent (ii) Adult (iii) Child

These terms have nothing to do with the actual age of the person rather than refer to ego states is a distinctive source of behaviour.

Test Questions

1. What is career development?
2. Explain about Individual and Organisational career development.
3. What is self development and how many form it has?
4. What are the stages of self-development?
5. What do you mean by management development and its features?
6. What are the methods of management development?

CASES

Sierra Textiles Limited

Sierra Textiles Limited has witnessed upheavals in its business journey. It was initiated by Mr. Arora in the year 1986 with its plant in Kolkata. Today it brags of 4 plants in Kolkata alone. It has a whopping turnover being in the vicinity of 600 crores. It has technical expertise from a Korean giant and it is the supplier of Jeans the company has been facing vagaries but it has retained its position as one of the leading companies in the Textile sector. The company has the mix of young and experienced operative manpower the old and new Technology is manning this Textiles industry.

Mr. Bipul Mehra, son of the founder of the Textiles industry, is concerned at the colossal investment on the latest Technology automation computerization and recruitment of Qualified manpower. The training of workers, supervisors and managerial manpower has been carried out by fits and starts.

Mr. Vijay heads the Eastern Region. The upgradation of Technical skills was the dire need for the company. He opines that new technology made it necessity the immediate skill upgradation of the old workers and educating new entrants.

Mr. Ram who heads the Western Regional Head points out that the customers especially the foreign buyers are demanding product Quality. Mr. Ashok the head of the personnel department is exposing manpower to Quality improvement programmes.

Mr. Sinha who heads the Southern Region is emphatic on training policy and skilled personnels.

Mr. Mehra opines— I am of the opinion that a company like our should groom men with its own premises away from the workplace.

Mr. Bhandari is of the opinion that 'I am open to the idea of satisfying the direct need of training in the company.

1. Develop a model of a Training system in the company.
2. Do you feel a Training Institute would help in meeting the training needs of Sierra Textiles Ltd. Give reasons.
3. Which type of research work can be successfully earned out in an institute attached to a corporate entity as the one encouraged by Bipul Mehra?

Allahabad Bank

The Allahabad Bank was incorporated in 1958 with its Head Office at Mumbai. It has mushroomed all over India. It is one of the well-staffed banks in the country. The Bank has set up Regional Offices in Metropolis. The strength of its employees has shot up immensely with the nationalisation of Banks, this Bank has re-oriented its policies. Crash programmes have been introduced. This Bank has been allotted many districts in Punjab, Bihar, Chennai, Madhya Pradesh and Uttar Pradesh. This Bank is giving a lead to other Banks in states. Each Branch is doing a commendable job in giving loans to poor farmers. It is financing the people to better their miserable lot. In the agricultural field its job is remarkable indeed. The businessmen have profited from this bank.

The comprehensive corporate reorganisation plan has been introduced to cope with problems stemming from the growth and diversification process. The reorganisation ushered a change in duties at various levels. There is a functional division at the Head Office and Regional Offices. The area and branch offices handled all aspects. A large number of technical officers such as Engineers and Agricultural Officers, Accountants and Managers have been recruited to look after manpower planning, recuitment, training and evaluations.

The Bank achieves rural penetration and it is eradicating regional imbalances.

This bank is growing and spreading its tentacles in the remote areas. The managers are trying to hike deposits in their Banks.

The Staffing, Evaluation and Career Efflorescence

The total staff has gone up from Lakhs to Crores. The hierarchical levels range from Grade E to Grade A Special in the officer category.

The Bank has dispersed geographically in large states and districts with many employees.

The Method of Training in Bank

The training function was impressive indeed. Since a large number of persons have been recruited their training activities must be stepped up to give excellent and prompt services to customers.

The clerical and subordinate staffs were manning the different branches. The Bank had to bank on the job-training. There was a stupendous spurt in expansion activities. It was trying to relieve a good employee for attending training courses, 'unwanted staff' got sent for training event it resulted in waste of time.

Mr. Kumar tookover the charge of manpower developments.

The faculty work was a deviation from the normal career path and hence it was difficult to get competent people with a flair for teaching.

Requirement for Prospective Plan for Training.

Mr. Prashad was preparing a perspective plan for training and he supported for training required from officers at various level.

Questions

1. What are the training need of Allahabad Bank?
2. What are the obstacle faced by Mr. Kumar and why?
3. Prepare a blueprint of recommendations for training in Allahabad Bank.

Crisis in Industries

The Sona Limited is a colossal public sector company which produces fertilisers, this company has established the fertiliser unit in the remote backward rural areas as per govt. directives. The company keeps in mind the uplift of the poor masses of the area. Hence it has recruited semi-skilled and unskilled employees from the villages and town. The local workers constitute the major chunk in the company.

The company has sophisticated technology in the output of fertilisers. The company follows the policy to hire engineers from recognised institutions as Management Trainees and to train them for Junior Management Cadre. The Junior Management of the unit comprises around 100 young engineers. The company has residential colony for employees near the factory.

At the outset the relations between the Junior Managers and workers were not cordial. The indiscipline on the part of workers was discernible. But the complaint was brushed aside to evade industrial problems. This stand of the senior managers threw cold water on the enthusiasm of Junior Engineers. They began to look for jobs elsewhere. In the past the turn over of young experienced engineers was high, which gave anxious moments to the management. The performance of the company was not satisfactory as the production of fertilisers was obstructed thanks to technical limitations.

When the situation took a worse turn the untoward incident occurred in the bagging plant. A junior technical engineer Mr. Bose was entrusted with the task of repairing and maintaining a bagging machine to be finished within a week—by the plant manager who Chafed under onerous pressure, thanks to technical problems of his area. Three days after the assignment of the job, Mr. Bose found the progress satisfactory behind plans and it was owing to the casual stance of workers under his baton. On the fourth day he called all his employees on the shop-floor and explained the unsatisfactory progress of the job. He also went on to explain the cause of delay, uttering how it was a sine-qua-non in the interest of the company and all workers ought to keep their heads down and to finish their assigned tasks in time.

One of the workers Mr. Saha the union leader put forth issues like production incentives overtime, canteen services quality etc. which were not properly attended to by the management. If the company turns Nelson's eye to the demands of workers the workers should not bother about the company's interest.

Mr. Bose reported that these things should be looked into by the Junior Managers and the workers could not invent excuse for delaying a job. Mr. Bose's remark had no impact and the workers under him began with their casual approach with the backing of Mr. Saha. While reporting facts to the Plant Manager. Mr. Bose was asked to release a letter of warning to Mr. Saha. Mr. Saha was given a letter of warning after reading, which he started hurling invectives at Mr. Bose threatening him with the direct consequences. This was noticed by junior engineers in the plant and workers on shop-floor. Being enraged Mr. Bose reported the incident to the Plant Manager who gave him assurance to look into the matter.

All junior engineers thronged in the colony and decided to cease work. Mr. Saha was sacked. All Junior engineers gathered at the factory gate and informed the G.M. of their decision. The H.R. Manager explained that no worker be sacked without an enquiry. The G.M. asked the H.R. Manager for issuance of suspension orders. Mr. Saha was put under suspension pending the enquiry.

The union representatives met the G.M. demanding withdrawal of suspension orders failing which they threatened to go on strike. The G.M. urgently convened a meeting of senior managers to pursue the matter. The majority was of the opinion that strike at this stage would administer severe setback to the company which is plagued by crisis and the top priority should be given to continue production and this warding of strike, they were of the opinion that Junior engineers could be persuaded to resume their duties by giving assurance of non-recurrence of such an untoward incident.

What are the pros and cons of new technology in an industry?

3. Answer the following questions

The General manager obliged the majority & the suspension order issued to Mr. Saha.

(i) Was the decision taken by the G.M. Justified?

(ii) What will be the result of the G.M.'s decision?

(iii) What decision would you have taken as G.M.?

Technological Grooming Inc

Technological Grooming Inc has been sponsored to generate and distribute videotaped courses lectures. The market experience forms a firm belief with Mr. John president of the company that the demand for his product would not justify operations. A buries of lectures for one course had been engendered, but sales of it were disconcerting. Students who watched the Tapes chorused that they preferred a live teacher even though he were not savy as the video lectures.

Mr. John had invested $ 30,000 from his funds and had spent a year as full timer for the company. He concluded that he would dismantle the company he could not recover his $ 30,000 and he took decision that further investments would be quite unfair.

(1) Two conditions are must in biological and social system for innovations- 'New species organism or organisation that servives.

First a mutation (novel system) second an ambience buttressing the mutation. Catalogues the disaster of the company in ecological biological analogs terms.

(1) Delineate the resources Technological Grooming Inc. has been taken from its environment and how its outputs are prized by the environment where did this interaction collapse, triggering the failure of the company.

(2) What steps might Mr. John take to make his ambience more supportive of his organisation? Do you think he could be crowned with success? Why?

Computer Revolution

Mr. Bright heads the accounting section in a fast growing manufacturing company. In the section there are 50 employees under his control. The company has five hundred employees who are from nearby areas. The tremendous changes in Science and Technology have spurred management to introduce mechanization in the accounting section. Mr. Bright is asked to explicate the import of having a to his employees. The introduction of computer has affected all areas of life. Some twenty employees will have to restructure their job responsibilities, ten employees need grooming in the handling of computers and the remaining ten may have to knock at the doors of other companies for jobs.

The scenario is akin to another situation visualized by Mr. Bright some time back six months ago the company procured a computer on a leaşe basis to handle the production inventory. The management is pleased with the arrangement for the inventory processing has improved tremendously. But unfortunately the production propel have resisted the step vehemently. Mr. Bright is in straits. Strange enough he is given the responsibility of introducing the computer in his own section.

Question :

1. Suppose, you are head of the particular unit and you are consigned to install computer, how would you manage to inform your subordinates about the proposed change and make them favourable?

Better Pay Scale for Welders

A line manager was appointed the chief of personnel in a public sector undertaking which had an upheavals in the past. The line manager had to enter into a wage agreement with the worker's union after accepting the assignment within a year. The union at that time was predominated by the non-technical staff. The union's charter of demands catered to the very interest of its dominating member groups. It demanded a striking revision in gardener's pay scale but was not voliferating the hike in the pay scale of workers in technical grades.

The union members raised an argument that the job of the gardeners is mementous to keep up the ambience and greenery in front of the factory. The workers of the factory can inhale fresh air in the sprawling lawn after their staffs are over and then they may repair to their homes. The role of welders is not that important because they acquire their routine jobs within the premises of the factory. Gardeners on the other hand have to perform their respective work in the open area, which allows the rays of the sun and showers of rain.

The management bows to these demands of union since the union extend cordial co-operation within inconsonance with the burden of the pay revision guidances of the Company. When agreement was signed and when it was communicated by management and the union in the respective manner there was a chance of protests from the technical staffs. They staged a walkout of the union and staged a march round the company crying hoarse. Hire grass cutters get more pay than gas cutters.

In the engineering assembly union till there is an implementation of revised pay scale welding was conceived to be a highly rated job. But not for a larger lease of time.

1. What may happen if welders get more pay than their competitors.?
2. Assess the pros and cons of the approach of the management and the union?
3. Suggests a way expected beyond the problem.

ABCL Limited

ABCL seeks a young smart men with oodtles of dynamism and energy to work as a salesman whose basic task is to sell off its product line to retail stores. They should have the tact and acumen to talk to customers and speak eloquently and fluently about the products of the company.

They should have knack to meet and handle different sorts of people and they should have accuracy to transfer orders to order forms.

Mr. Vikas the H. R. Manager will interview the applicant's for the Salesman's job is having an application of one Mr. Prasad with the following details :

Age	:	22 years
Academic qualification	:	Graduated with Hons in Chemistry
Marital Status	:	Bachelor
Work experience	:	Held two jobs Served as lab. assistant in hospital and worked as a chemist in a Medicine Firm.

1. Being an expert, what will be your goal for interviewing? How would you phrase your questions?
2. Is Mr. Prasad a suitable candidate for the job? Give reasons for your opinion, on the basis of information provided about the candidate.

Bibliography

A-Books

Alexander, K.C. : Participative Management-The Indian Experience. Shri Ram Centre for Industrial Relations, New Delhi, 1973.

Armstrong, Michael : Handbook of Personnel Management, Kogam Page, London, 1976.

Allen Louis : Management and Organisation, p. 119.

Basu, K.S. : New Dimensions in Personnel Management. Mcmillan, New Delhi. 1979.

Beach, Dale S : Personnel, Macmillan Publishing Co. New York.

British Institute of Management, Job Evaluation-A Practical Guide, London.

Byars Loyd R. and L.W. Rue, : Human Resource and Personnel Management, Richard D. Irwin, Illinois, 1984.

Chatterjee, N.N. : Management of Personnel in Indian Enterprises, Allied Book Agency, New Delhi, 1978.

Cox, Robert J. : Workers Participation in Management, International Institute of Labour Studies, Geneva, 1967.

Coleman, Bruce P. : An Integrated System of Manpower Planning, Business Horizon, Vol. 13, 1970, p. 89.

Devis, Keith, : Human Behaviour at Work, Tata McGraw Hill, New Delhi, 1985.

Drucker, Peter F. : Management-Tasks, Responsibilities Practices, Allied Publishers Pvt. Ltd., Mumbai-1975, p. 100.

Durbin, A. J., : Personnel and Human Resource Management, D. Van Northland Co., New York, 1981.

Dwivedi, R. S. : Management of Human Resources, Oxford & IBH, New Delhi, 1980.

Employers' Federation of India, Fringe Benefits in Indian Industry, Bombay, 1972.

Flippo,Edwin B. : Personnel Management, McGraw Hill, Kogakusha, Tokyo, 1990.

Ghosh, S. : Trade Unionism in Underdeveloped Countries, Bookland, Calcutta, 1966.

Giri, V. V. : Labour Problems in Indian Industry, Asia Publishing House, Bombay, 1972.

Gupta, C.G. : Managerial and Executive Remuneration in India, Allied Publishers, New Delhi, 1984.

Halder, S. K. : Evolution of Labour Management Relations and the Law of Industrial Disputes, Calcutta, 1953.

Halloran, Jack : Personnel and Human Resource Management, Prentice Hall Inc; New Jersy, 1986.

How to manage byresult, American Management Association, New York, 1967, p.15.

Indian Institute of Personnel Management, Readings in Personnel Management, Orient Longman, New Delhi, 1970.

International Labour Organisation, Labour Management Relations, (Report No. 23) Geneva, 1960.

Kappor,T.N. (ed) : Personnel Management and Industrial Relations in Indian N.M. Tripathi & Sons, Bombay, 1968.

Kudchedkar,L.S. : Aspects of Personnel Management and Industrial Relations, McGraw Hill, New York, 1979.

Koontz Herold & Cyril O'Donnell, Management, McGraw Hill, Tokyo, p. 161.

Kuch, T.J. : Personnel Administration and Appraisal, McGraw Hill, 1955.

Mathis, Robert L. and J.H.Jackson, Personnel Human Resource Management, West Publishing Co., New York, 1982.

Miner, Jon B. and M.G. Miner, Personnel and Industrial Relations Mcmillan Publishing Co., New York, 1977.

Monappa, Arun : Human Resource Planning and Career Planning, Ahmedabad (Mimeo).

Monappa, A. and : Personnel Management, Tata McGraw Hill,

M.S. Saiyidain, New Delhi, 1993.

Myers, CharlesA : Industrial Relations in India, Asia Publishing House, Bombay, 1970.

Prasad, L. : Personnel Management and Industrial Relations in Public Sector, Progressive Corporation, Bombay, 1973.

Singh, N.K. : Dimensions of Personnel Management, Vikas Publishing House, New Delhi, 1984.

Singh, N.K. and G.K. Suri (eds), : Personnel Management, Vikas Publishing House, New Delhi, 1985.

Srivastava Suresh (ed.), : Behavioural Sciences in Management, Asia Publishing House, Bombay, 1967.

Yoder, Dale : Personnel Management and Industrial Relations, Prentice Hall of India, New Delhi, 1977.

Yoder, Dale and H.G. Heneman : Handbook of Personnel and Industrial Relations, Bureau of National Affairs, Washington, 1979.B-Journals HRD Newsletter, XLRI Jamshed. Industrial and Labour Relations, Cornell University, U.S.A. Industrial Relations, Institute of Industrial Relations, University of California, Berkley U.S.A Industrial Management, Industrial Management, Society Chicago, U.S.; Indian Journal of Psychology, New Delhi. Indian Journal of Social Work, Tata Institute of Social Sciences, Bombay. Indian Journal of Training and Development, Indian Society for Training and Development, New Delhi. Labour Chronicle, Bombay.

C-Reports : Report of the Labour Investigation Committee, 1946. Report of the National Commission on Labour, 1969. Report of the Bhoothalingam Committee on Wages, Incomes and Prices, 1979.

Index

D

E

F

P

Q

R